AN

INTRODUCTORY GRAMMAR

OF THE

GERMAN LANGUAGE,

WITH

EXERCISES FOR WRITING GERMAN,

USED IN

THE CAMBERWELL COLLEGIATE SCHOOL,
THE BLACKHEATH NEW PROPRIETARY SCHOOL,
AND OTHER SCHOOLS.

BY

THE REV. J. G. TIARKS, PH. DR.

MINISTER OF THE GERMAN PROTESTANT REFORMED CHURCH IN LONDON.

LONDON:

J. SOUTER, SCHOOL LIBRARY, 132, FLEET-STREET;
B. FELLOWS, LUDGATE-HILL; BLACK AND ARMSTRONG,
8, WELLINGTON-STREET, NORTH, STRAND;
J. WACEY, 4, OLD BROAD-STREET.

1837.

299.

LONDON :
PRINTED BY JOHN WERTHEIMER AND CO.
CIRCUS PLACE, FINSBURY CIRCUS.

PREFACE.

My object in publishing this little work is, to furnish a Grammar which contains nothing but the elements of the German Language according to my system. It is an abstract of my "Practical Grammar of the German Language." However useful those who wish to acquire an accurate knowledge of the German, may find the latter, it contains too much for young students who are instructed in large classes. For such this abstract is intended; and as I' have added Exercises for Writing German, with copies of the handwriting, most beautifully executed, I hope it will be found to answer the purpose for which it is intended.

JOH. GERH. TIARKS.

67, Great Prescot-street, Goodman's Fields.

May, 1837.

37.

299.

GERMAN.		ENGLISH.		NAME.
S	ſ, s, ſſ, ß, ſt	S	f, s, ſſ, sz, st	Ess, ess-ess, ess-tset, ess-tey
T	t	T	t	Tey
U	u	U	u	Oo
V	v	V	v	Fou
W	w	W	w	Vey
X	x	X	x	Iks
Y	y	Y	y	Ypsilon
Z	z, tz	Z	z, tz	Tset, Tey-tset

THE SIMPLE VOWELS.

A, a.   E, e.   I, i.   O, o.   U, u.   Y, y.

THE MODIFIED VOWELS.

Ae, ä (like *a* in *fate*).   Oe, ö (like the French *eu* in *peu*). Ue, ü (like the French *u* in *fut*).

THE DIPHTHONGS.

Au, au (like *ou* in *house*).   Ei, ei or Ey, ey (like *i* in *kite*).   Eu, eu (like *oi* in *point*).   Aeu, äu nearly the same as Eu, eu.   Ai, ai, Ay, ay, Oi, oi, Oy, oy, only occur in foreign words.

Note 1.—The consonants b and d sound at the end of words, like p and t.

Note 2.—The vowel i is made long by the addition of e; as, ie, die, or by the insertion of h: as, ihn. The other vowels are made long by the insertion of h; as, Bahn, Lehre, Sohn, Huhn. If there is a t in the word, this h is always joined to it; as, Thal, Roth, Muth.

Note 3.—The capital Y does not occur in any German word; the small one is used in German words only as a final letter with e, ey; but most authors have rejected it altogether, except in words of Greek origin.

Pronounce the following Words.

Band, Baum, kaum, mein, dein, sein, bienen, Bienen, Miene, Weise, Wiese, Eule, heute, beuten, Leute; Hände, Wände; Aeste; Völker, Götter; böse; Mühe, Mühle, müssen; äußern; Sohn, Söhne, Gang, Gänge; Volk, Boden; Dieb, gieb; Ruß, muß, nuß, Nutzen; putzen, für; fühlen, sich, sehen; mögen, wägen, Zeit, Zank, zeigen, ziehen; faulen, saugen, Alter, Kummer, Runde, Nonne; heben, beben, behende, Loch, hoch, Stock, Stück; stechen, Fenster; Töne; voll, wollen, Knabe, Gnade, kneten; Knie; Quelle, Jahr, jung; Gesicht, Aussicht, Schule, schön, schon; Wolke, Wunder, Mund, weil, viel, seyn; sehen; wachsen, Christen.

THE ARTICLES.

	Definite.				Indefinite.	
	SING.		PLUR.		SING.	
	Masc.	Fem.	Neut.		Masc.	Fem.	Neut.
N.	der	die	das.	die	N. ein	eine	ein
G.	des	der	des.	der	G. eines	einer	eines
D.	dem	der	dem.	den	D. einem	einer	einem
A.	den	die	das.	die	A. einen	eine	ein

Observe that the definite article denotes the three genders in the nominative, and that the masculine of the indefinite articles is the same as the neuter.

DECLENSION OF SUBSTANTIVES.

The first Declension

comprehends all the substantives of the feminine gender. The singular remains unaltered. The plural is formed by adding n or en to the singular. Original monosyllables and those ending in niß, only take e in the plural, and modify the vowels a o u into ä, ö, ü. The dative plur. always ends in n in all the declensions. All substantives have a capital initial.

Examples.

	Sing.	Plur.

N. die Schale, the saucer.   die Schalen, the saucers.
G. der Schale, of the saucer.   der Schalen, of the saucers.
D. der Schale, to the saucer.   den Schalen, to the saucers.
A. die Schale, the saucer.   die Schalen, the saucers.

N. die Gabel, the fork.   die Gabeln, the forks.
G. der Gabel, of the fork.   der Gabeln, of the forks.
D. der Gabel, to the fork.   den Gabeln, to the forks.
A. die Gabel, the fork.   die Gabeln, the forks.

N. die Tugend, the virtue.   die Tugenden, the virtues.
G. der Tugend, of the virtue.   der Tugenden, of the virtues.
D. der Tugend, to the virtue.   den Tugenden, to the virtues.
A. die Tugend, the virtue.   die Tugenden, the virtues.

N. die Hand, the hand.   die Hände, the hands.
G. der Hand, of the hand.   der Hände, of the hands.
D. der Hand, to the hand.   den Händen, to the hands.
A. die Hand, the hand.   die Hände, the hands.

Note 1.—The plural of die Mutter, the mother, and die Tochter, the daughter, is die Mütter, die Töchter.

Note 2.—The following originally ended in e, and therefore do not belong to the *original* monosyllables, which make the plural to end in e, and modify the three vowels, a, o, u; die Art, the kind; die Brut, the brood; die Bucht, the bay; die Burg, the castle; die Cur, the cure; die Fahrt, the conveyance; die Flur, the field; die Fluth, the flood; die Form, the form; die Fracht, the freight; die Frau, the woman; die Last, the burden; die Mark, the mark; die Pflicht, the duty; die Post, the post; die Quaal, the torment; die Schaar, the crowd; die Schlacht, the battle; die Schrift, the writing; die Schuld, the debt; die Spur, the trace; die That, the deed; die Tracht, the

mode of dress ; bie Trift, the pasture ; bie Uhr, the watch ;
bie Wahl, the choice ; bie Welt, the world; bie Zahl, the
number ; bie Zeit, the time. The plural of these ends in
en ; bie Art, bie Arten.

The second Declension

comprehends all substantives of the masculine and
neuter genders ending in the unaccented syllables el, en,
and er, and the diminutives formed by the syllables chen
and lein.

The gen. sing. is formed by adding ß to the nominative, and the dat. plur. by adding n, (except in those
which end in en).

In the plural of several words, a o u are modified into
ä, ö, ü.

Examples.

Sing.	Plur.
N. ber Vogel, the bird.	bie Vögel, the birds.
G. bes Vogels, of the bird.	ber Vögel, of the birds.
D. bem Vogel, to the bird.	ben Vögeln, to the birds.
A. ben Vogel, the bird.	bie Vögel, the birds.
N. ber Garten, the garden.	bie Gärten, the gardens.
G. bes Gartens, of the garden.	ber Gärten, of the gardens.
D. bem Garten, to the garden.	ben Gärten, to the gardens.
A. ben Garten, the garden.	bie Gärten, the gardens.
N. bas Messer, the knife.	bie Messer, the knives.
G. bes Messers, of the knife.	ber Messer, of the knives.
D. bem Messer, to the knife.	ben Messern, to the knives.
A. bas Messer, the knife.	bie Messer, the knives.

Note 1.—The following take n in the plural, ber
Pantoffel, the slipper ; ber Gevatter, the godfather; ber
Stachel, the sting; ber Stiefel, the boot; ber Vetter, the
cousin ; bie Pantoffeln, Gevattern, Stacheln, Stiefeln, Vettern.

Note 2.—Diminutives, formed by lein and chen, are used to express not only littleness, but also fondness, ridicule, and contempt: as, das Knäblein, das Söhnchen. They are all of the neuter gender.

Note 3. — The following change a, o, u, in the plural into ä, ö, ü, der Apfel, the apple; der Acker, the field; der Bruder, the brother; der Faden, the thread; der Garten, the garden; der Graben, the ditch; der Hafen, the haven; der Hammel, the wether; der Hammer, the hammer; der Handel, the affair; der Laden, the shop; der Mangel, the want; der Nabel, the navel; der Sattel, the saddle; der Schnabel, the beak; der Schwager, the brother-in-law; der Vater, the father; der Vogel, the bird.

The Third Declension

originally contained all substantives of the masculine gender ending in e; but many words have lost the final e, and end now in a consonant. All the cases singular and plural are formed by adding n or en to the nominative singular. One neuter, das Herz, the heart, the accusative of which is like the nominative, belongs to this declension.

Sing.	Plur.
N. der Falke, the falcon.	die Falken, the falcons.
G. des Falken, of the falcon.	der Falken, of the falcons.
D. dem Falken, to the falcon.	den Falken, to the falcons.
A. den Falken, the falcon.	die Falken, the falcons.
N. der Mensch, the human being.	die Menschen.
G. des Menschen, of the human being.	der Menschen.
D. dem Menschen, to the human being.	den Menschen.
A. den Menschen, the human being.	die Menschen.

Note 1.— The following words have lost the final e, and therefore belong to this declension: der Advocat, the

lawyer; der Aſtronom, the astronomer; der Bär, the bear; der Barbar, the barbarian; der Conſonant, the consonant; der Antagoniſt, the antagonist; der Chriſt, the Christian; der Demagog, the demagogue; der Ducat, the ducat; der Elephant, the elephant; der Fürſt, the prince; der Geograph, the geographer; der Geſell, the companion: der Graf, the count; der Herr, the master; der Held, the hero; der Hirt, the herdsman; der Huſar, the hussar; der Idiot, the idiot; der Jeſuit, the Jesuit; der Katholik, the Roman Catholic; der Klient, the client; der Monarch, the monarch; der Mohr, the moor; der Methodiſt, the methodist; der Narr, the fool; der Patient, the patient; der Ochs, the ox; der Patriarch, the patriarch; der Philoſoph, the philosopher; der Planet, the planet; der Poet, the poet; der Prälat, the prelate; der Prinz, the prince: der Proteſtant, the protestant; der Quadrant, the quadrant; der Soldat, the soldier; der Student, the student; der Theolog, the theologian; der Thor, the fool; der Tyrann, the tyrant; der Ungar, the Hungarian; der Vorfahr, the ancestor.

Note 2.—The following formerly ended in en, and therefore, have ens in the genitive sing.; der Friede, the peace; der Funke, the spark; der Fußtapfe, the footstep; der Gedanke, the thought; der Glaube, the faith; der Haufe, the crowd; der Karpfe, the carp; der Name, the name; der Saame, the seed; der Schade, the damage; der Wille, the will; das Herz, the heart: as, des Friedens, des Herzens.

The fourth Declension

contains all the masculines and neuters which do not belong to the second and third. Neither a feminine nor a masculine ending in el, en, er, or e, nor a neuter ending in el, en, er, can belong to this declension. Neuters not ending in el, en, er, must belong to it. Masculines not ending in el, en, er, or e, may belong to the third or fourth. The list of words given under the third and fourth declension, wil! greatly assist the student in ascertaining this.

The genitive sing. ends in eß, the dative in e, (which is often omitted), the accusative is like the nominative. The plural of most ends in e; but several neuters, especially those of one syllable, and a few masculines have er in the plural. Many change a o u into å, ŏ, ů, in the plural.

	Sing.	Plur.
N.	der Tiſch, the table.	die Tiſche, the tables.
G.	des Tiſches, of the table.	der Tiſche, of the tables.
D.	dem Tiſche, to the table.	den Tiſchen, to the tables.
A.	den Tiſch, the table.	die Tiſche, the tables.
N.	das Thal, the valley.	die Thåler, the valleys.
G.	des Thales, of the valley.	der Thåler, of the valleys.
D.	dem Thale, to the valley.	den Thålern, to the valleys.
A.	das Thal, the valley.	die Thåler, the valleys.
N.	der Geiſt, the spirit.	die Geiſter, the spirits.
G.	des Geiſtes, of the spirit.	der Geiſter, of the spirits.
D.	dem Geiſte, to the spirit.	den Geiſtern, to the spirits.
A.	den Geiſt, the spirit.	die Geiſter, the spirits.

Note 1.—The following form the plural in er, and change a o u into å, ŏ, ů.

(a) Masculines : der Gott, a heathen idol ; der Geiſt, the spirit ; der Leib, the body ; der Mann, the man ; der Ort, the place ; der Rand, the edge ; der Vormund, the guardian; der Wald, the wood ; der Wurm, the worm ; der Böſewicht, the wicked wight, the villain.

(b) Neuters : das Aas, the carrion ; das Amt, the office; das Augenlied, the eyelid ; das Bad, the bath ; das Bild, the picture ; das Blatt, the leaf ; das Brett, the board ; das Buch, the book ; das Dach, the roof ; das Denkmal, the monument; das Dorf, the village; das Ey, the egg; das Fach, the department; das Faß, the cask; das Feld, the field; das Geld, the money; das Gemach, the apartment; das Gemüth, the mind; das Gespenst, the spectre; das Geschlecht, the race; das Glas, the glass; das Glied, the member; das Grab, the grave; das Grabmal, the tomb; das Gras, the grass; das Gut, the estate; das Haupt, the head; das Haus, the house; das Holz, the wood; das Hospital, the hospital; das Huhn, the fowl; das Kalb, the calf; das Kind, the child; das Kleid, the garment; das Korn, the grain; das Kraut, the herb; das Lamm, the lamb; das Licht, the light; das Lied, the song; das Loch, the hole; das Maul, the mouth; das Nest, the nest; das Pfand, the pledge; das Rad, the wheel; das Regiment, the regiment; das Schild, the sign of a house; das Schloß, the castle; das Schwerdt, the sword; das Spital, the hospital; das Thal, the valley; das Volk, the people; das Wamms, the jacket; das Weib, the wife.

(c) All those which end in thum; as, der Reichthum, riches; die Reichthümer.

Note 2.—The following masculines change a o u in the plural into â, ô, û, and form the plural in e; Abt, Abbruck, Alter, Anfang, Antrag, Arzt, Ast, Auftrag, Ausbruck, Ausgang, Bach, Balg, Ball, Band (the volume of a book) Bart, Bauch, Baum, Bischof, Block, Bock, Brand, Brauch, Bruch, Busch, Canal, Cardinal, Choral, Damm, Dampf, Darm, Diebstahl, Dunst, Einfluß, Eingang, Fall, Floh, Fluch, Flug, Fluß, Frosch, Fuchs, Fund, Fuß, Gang, Gast, Gebrauch, Geruch, Gesang, Grund, Fuß, Hahn, Hals, Hof, Huth, Kahn, Kampf, Kauf, Klang, Kloß, Klotz, Knopf, Koch, Kopf, Korb, Krampf, Kranz, Kropf, Krug, Kuß, Lauf, Markt, Marsch, Morast, Nachschuß, Napf, Pallast, Pabst, Paß, Pflock, Pflug, Platz, Probst, Rank, Rath, Raum, Rausch, Rock, Rumpf, Saal, Sack, Saft, Sarg, Satz, Saum, Schalk, Schutz, Schlag, Schlauch, Schlund, Schuß,

Schmaus, Schopf, Schrank, Schurz, Schuß, Schwamm, Schwan, Schwank, Schwanz, Schwung, Schwur, Sohn, Spaß, Spruch, Sprung, Stab, Stall, Stamm, Stand, Stock, Storch, Stoß, Strang, Strauch, Strom, Strumpf, Stuhl, Sturm, Sturz, Sumpf, Tanz, Thurm, Thon, Topf, Trank, Traum, Trog, Trumpf, Umstand, Vogt, Vorhang, Vorrath, Vorschlag, Vorschuß, Vorwand, Wall, Weinstock, Wolf, Wunsch, Wurf, Zahn, Zaum, Zahn, Zoll, Zopf, Zug, Zustand, Zwang.

Note 3 — The following form the singular after the fourth, but the plural after the third declension ; das Auge, pl. die Augen, der Affect, der Aspect, der Diamant ; das Ende, the end ; das Insect, der Mast, the mast ; das Leib, the sorrow ; der Lorbeer, the laurel ; das Ohr, the ear ; der Pfau, the peacock ; der Schmerz, the pain ; der See, the lake ; der Sporn, the spur ; der Staat, the state ; der Strahl, the ray ; der Strauß, the Ostrich ; der Thron, the throne ; der Unterthan, the subject ; der Zierrath, the ornament.

Note. 4.—The following masculines belong to the fourth declension.   Such as admit a plural, form it in e.

Aal, Abend, Abscheu, Anblick, Anstrich, Arm, Befehl, Begriff, Berg, Besitz, Besuch, Beweis, Bleistift, Blick, Blitz, Brief, Dienst, Dolch, Durst, Eid, Essig, Ehrgeiz, Feind, Fisch, Fleiß, Frembling, Freund, Frühling, Geiz, Gemahl, Gewinn, Grad, Gram, Greis, Halm, Haß, Häring, Hänfling, Hauch, Hecht, Herbst, Hirsch, Hochmuth, Huf, Hund, Jüngling, Käfig, Kaffee, Keil, Keim, Knoblauch, Kobold, Kohl, König, Krebs, Kreis, Lachs, Laib, Laut, Lehrling, Liebling, Luchs, Mond, Monat, Mord, Mund, Muth, Neid, Oheim, Pfad, Pfennig, Pilgrim, Plan, Preis, Prozeß, Putz, Ring, Rath, Salat, Schall, Scherz, Schmid, Schirm, Schnee, Schmetterling, Schritt, Schuh, Schlaf, Schweiß, Sonnenschirm, Sinn, Spinat, Sperling, Stahl, Staar, Staub, Stern, Stein, Stier, Stoff, Stroh, Streit, Stolz, Sultan, Thau, Tag, Thee, Theil, Tod, Trost, Trunken=

bolb, Unholb, Verstand, Vorwitz, Verkehr, Wahn, Weg, Wein, Wind, Witz, Zank, Ziel, Zweck.

Note 5.—Some have in the plural different terminations, according to a difference in signification : bas Bett, the bed, bie Bette, the beds, bie Betten, bedding ; bas Band, the bond, bie Bande, the fetters, bie Bänder, the ribbons ; bas Ding, the thing, bie Dinge, things generally ; bie Dinger, especially used of little children and animals ; bas Gesicht, the sight, the face, bie Gesichte, the visions ; bie Gesichter, the faces ; bas Horn, the horn, bie Horne, different kinds of horn, bie Hörner, the horns ; bas Land, the land, bie Lande, lands, countries in general ; bie Länder, individual countries ; ber Ort, the place, bie Orte, places in general; bie Oerter, individual places ; bas Stück, the piece, bie Stücke, the pieces, bie Stücken, the fragments ; bas Wort, the word, bie Worte, words in general forming a sentence, bie Wörter, single words.

Declension of Proper Names.

The inflection of proper names is indicated either by the definite article, or by the termination.

When the definite article is used, proper names remain unaltered in the singular : bie Gedichte bes Virgil, the poems of Virgil ; ber Bruder ber Marie, the brother of Mary.

When the definite article is not used, the names of females ending in e take n's in the genitive and n in the dative : Marien's Bruder, Karolinen's Schwester. Ich habe es Marien gegeben, I have given it to Mary.

The names of males ending in s, ß, sch, x, or z, take en's in the genitive (and in some provinces of Germany, en in the dative and accusative) : Bossen's Uebersetzungen, Fritzen's Bücher.

The names of males and females ending in other letters

than those above mentioned, take ß in the genitive: Heinrich, Heinrich's, Elisabeth, Elisabeth's.

Additional Remarks on the Declension of Substantives.

1. The following words expressing weight, measure, or number, are used only in the singular.

das Buch, the quire.	der Mann, the man.
das Bund, the bundle.	die Mark, the mark.
das Dutzend, the dozen.	das Paar, the pair.
das Faß, the cask.	das Pfund, the pound.
das Glas, the glass.	das Ries, the ream.
der Grad, the degree.	das Schock, three score.
das Klafter, the fathom.	das Stück, the piece.
das Loth, half an ounce.	das Zoll, the inch.
das Mal, the mark.	

2 The following feminines, and those which express a measure of time, such as Stunde, hour, Minute, minute, are excepted.

die Elle, the yard.	die Stunde, the league.
die Flasche, the bottle.	die Tasse, the cup.
die Meile, the mile.	die Unze, the ounce.

3. Those words, the measure, weight, or number, of which is expressed by the above mentioned substantives, are not put in the genitive, unless a part of a certain quantity or quality is meant; but in the same case with the preceding words: Sechs Buch Papier, six quires of paper; fünf Bund Stroh, five bundles of straw; zwölf Dutzend Aepfel, twelve dozens of apples; zehn Faß Bier, ten casks of beer; hundert Mann Reiterei, a hundred men cavalry; zwei Paar Schuhe, two pair of shoes; vier Pfund Zucker, four pounds of sugar; sechs Ellen-Tuch, six yards of cloth; zwei Glas Wein, two glasses of wine; drei Tassen

Kaffee, three cups of coffee; mein Freund schickte mir gestern zwei Flaschen alten Rheinwein, my friend sent me yesterday two bottles of old Rhenish wine. When only a part of a certain quantity or quality is meant, they are put in the genitive, or with the preposition von and the dative: sechs Pfund dieses Zuckers, or, von diesem Zucker, six pounds of this sugar.

Note.—All substantives ending in ei or ey, heit, keit, schaft, ung, ath, uth, are of the feminine gender.

THE DECLENSION OF ADJECTIVES.

Adjectives are not declined when used as predicates: der Mann ist gut, the man is good; die Frau ist gut, the woman is good; das Kind ist gut, the child is good; die Männer sind gut, die Frauen sind gut, die Kinder sind gut; das Kind wird groß, the child grows tall, die Kinder werden groß. When the adjective is used in an attributive sense, forming one notion with the substantive before which it stands, it is declined in three different ways, which we call the forms of inflection.

The First Form

is used when the adjective is not preceded by any article, pronoun, or numeral. In this form it has the following terminations.

	Sing.			Plur.
	Masc.	Fem.	Neut.	
N.	er.	e.	es.	e.
G.	es.	er.	es.	er.
D.	em.	er.	em.	en.
A.	en.	e.	es.	e.

	Sing.		
	Masc.	Fem.	Neut.
N.	guter Mann.	gute Frau.	gutes Kind.
G.	gutes Mannes.	guter Frau.	gutes Kindes.
D.	gutem Manne.	guter Frau.	gutem Kinde.
A.	guten Mann.	gute Frau.	gutes Kind.

c

Plur.

N. gute Männer.	gute Frauen.	gute Kinder.
G. guter Männer.	guter Frauen.	guter Kinder.
D. guten Männern.	guten Frauen.	guten Kindern.
A. gute Männer.	gute Frauen.	gute Kinder.

The Second Form

is used when the adjective is preceded by the definite article, or such pronouns and indefinite numerals which, like the definite article, indicate the three genders in the nominative: as, dieſer, dieſe, dieſes, this; jeder, jede, jedes, every, each. In this form the repetition of r. s. m. is avoided for the sake of euphony. The declension is as follows :—

Sing.

Masc.	*Fem.*	*Neut.*
N. der gute Mann.	die gute Frau.	das gute Kind.
G. des guten Mannes.	der guten Frau.	des guten Kindes.
D. dem guten Manne.	der guten Frau.	dem guten Kinde.
A. den guten Mann.	die gute Frau.	das gute Kind.

Plur.

N. die guten Männer.	Frauen.	Kinder.
G. der guten Männer.	Frauen.	Kinder.
D. den guten Männern.	Frauen.	Kindern.
A. die guten Männer.	Frauen.	Kinder.

Note.—Most authors drop the n in the nom. and acc. plur. after welche, which; ſolche, such; einige, ettiche, some; keine, no; viele, many; wenige, few; alle, all; mehrere, several; manche, many; as, alle gute Menſchen.

The Third Form

is used when the adjective is preceded by the indefinite article, ein, eine, ein, or the definite numeral Ein, Eine, Ein, or the indefinite numeral ein, eine, ein, or a possessive pronoun, mein, dein, fein, unfer, euer, ihr, or the personal pronouns, ich, du, wir, ihr, fie; none of which indicate the masc. and neut. gender in the nominative. The declension is as follows:

Sing.

	Masc.	Fem.	Neut.
N.	ein guter Mann.	eine gute Frau.	ein gutes Kind.
G.	eines guten Mannes.	einer guten Frau.	eines guten Kindes.
D.	einem guten Manne.	einer guten Frau.	einem guten Kinde.
A.	einen guten Mann.	eine gute Frau.	ein gutes Kind.

Plur.

		Fem.	Neut.
N.	meine guten Männer.	Frauen.	Kinder.
G.	meiner guten Männer.	Frauen.	Kinder.
D.	meinen guten Männern.	Frauen.	Kindern.
A.	meine guten Männer.	Frauen.	Kinder.

Note 1.—Adjectives are, in German, frequently used substantively, but declined like adjectives: der Gelehrte, des Gelehrten; ein Gelehrter, eines Gelehrten.

Note 2.—Adjectives ending in el, en, er, generally lose e, when they are declined: der Mann ist edel, the man is noble; der eble Mann, den edeln Mann.

Note 3.—When hoch, high, is declined, it changes ch into h: das hohe Haus.

Note 4.—Participles are declined like adjectives: geliebt, loved; ein geliebtes Kind, das geliebte Kind; der liebende Vater.

The Comparison of Adjectives.

The comparative is formed by adding er (only r, when the adjective ends in e), and the superlative by adding est (only st, when the adjective ends in e) to the positive.

The *e* before ſt is *generally* dropped in the superlative, when the adjective does not end in b, t, ð, ß, ſch, z, ſt.

   pos. ſchön, handsome; *comp.* ſchöner; *sup.* ſchönſt.

   — enge, narrow;   — enger;   — engſt.

   — wild, wild;   —, wilder;   — wildeſt.

   — ſüß, sweet;   — ſüßer;   — ſüßeſt.

The vowels a, o, u are, in many words, changed into å, ö, ü, in the comp. and sup.; as, arm, poor, comp. ärmer, sup. ärmſt; kurz, short, comp. kürzer, sup. kürzeſt.

The following words retain their original vowels: blaß, pale; bunt, variegated; fahl, fallow; fade, insipid; falſch, false; flach, flat; froh, joyful; gerade, straight; glatt, smooth; hohl, hollow; hold, kind; kahl, bald; karg, stingy; knapp, tight; lahm, lame; laß, tired; loſe, loose; matt, wearied; morſch, brittle, rotten; nackt, naked; platt, flat; plump, clumsy; roh, raw; rund, round; ſacht, gentle; ſanft, mild, gentle; ſatt, satisfied; ſchlaff, loose, lax; ſchlank, slender; ſchroff, rugged; ſtarr, stiff; ſtolz, proud; ſtraff, stiff, tight; ſtumm, dumb; ſtumpf, blunt; toll, mad; voll, full; zahm, tame.

Adjectives ending in el, en, er, generally lose *e* before l, n, r, in the comparative: as, edel, comp. edler; and the superlative of groß, is contracted into größt.

The comparative and superlative are declined like the positive: as, 1st form, ſchönerer Garten, 2nd form, der ſchönere Garten, 3rd form, ein ſchönerer Garten; gen. ſchöneres Gartens, des ſchöneren Gartens, eines ſchöneren Gartens, &c.; der ſchönſte Garten, mein ſchönſter Garten.

The superlative of eminence is expressed by ſehr, äußerſt, höchſt: as, dieſes iſt ein äußerſt ſchönes Haus, this is a most beautiful house.

When the superlative is used as a predicate without the definite article, it is expressed by am with the dative: as, dieſe Blume iſt am ſchönſten, this flower is most beautiful.

The comparative is formed by mehr, the superlative by am mehrsten or am meisten, 1. when different qualities of the same object are compared: der Mann ist mehr lustig als traurig, the man is more merry than sad. 2. In those adjectives which are used as predicates only and never inflected: abhold, averse; angst, anxious; anheischig, pledged by promise; bereit, ready; feind, hostile; gar, done, boiled enough; gänge und gæbe, current; eingebenk, mindful; uneingedenk, unmindful; getrost, of good cheer; gewärtig, aware; gram, bearing animosity; habhaft, in possession of; irre, wrong; kund, known; leid, distressing; noth, needful; nütze, useful; quitt, rid of; theilhaft, participating; verlustig, having forfeited.

The following are irregular:

Gut, good.	comp.	besser, better.	sup.	best, am besten.	
Viel, much.	—	mehr, more.	—	meist, am meisten or am mehrsten.	
Hoch, high.	—	höher, higher.	—	höchst, am höchsten.	
Nahe, near.	—	näher, nearer.	—	nächst, am nächsten.	

THE NUMERALS.

1. THE CARDINAL NUMBERS.

1, ein; 2, zwei; 3, drei; 4, vier; 5, fünf; 6, sechs; 7, sieben; 8, acht; 9, neun; 10, zehn; 11, elf or eilf; 12, zwölf; 13, dreizehn; 14, vierzehn; 15, fünfzehn; 16, sechszehn; 17, siebenzehn or siebzehn; 18, achtzehn; 19, neunzehn; 20, zwanzig; 21, ein und zwanzig; 22, zwei und zwanzig, &c. &c.; 30, dreißig; 40, vierzig; 50, fünfzig; 60, sechszig; 70, siebenzig or siebzig; 80, achtzig; 90, neunzig; 100, hundert; 101, hundert und ein, &c.; 200, zwei hundert, &c.; 1000, tausend; 10,000, zehn tausend; a million, eine Million.

Note 1.—The units always precede the tens, ein und zwanzig; fünf und achtzig.

Note 2.—Ein, eine, ein, is declined like the indefinite

article. When preceded by the definite article or a pronoun, it is declined like an adjective: ber Eine; bie Eine, bas Eine, biefes Eine; gen. bes Einen, biefes Einen. When it is used substantively, without an article or pronoun, it has the termination of the first form of inflection of the adjectives: Einer, Eine, Eines; Einer ber Männer, Eine ber Frauen; Eines ber Kinder. Zwei and brei take the terminations of the gen. and dat. cases: zweier, zweien, when the cases of the words to which they belong are not indicated by the termination.

2. THE ORDINAL NUMBERS.

1st, ber erfte; 2nd, ber zweite; 3rd, ber britte; 4th, ber vierte; 5th, ber fünfte; 6th, ber fechfte; 7th, ber fiebente or fiebte; 8th, ber achte; 9th, ber neunte; 10th, ber zehnte; 11th, ber elfte or eilfte; 12th, ber zwölfte; 13th, ber breizehnte; 14th, ber vierzehnte; 15th, ber fünfzehnte; 16th, ber fechszehnte; 17th, ber fiebenzehnte; 18th, ber achtzehnte; 19th, ber neunzehnte; 20th, ber zwanzigfte; 21st, ber ein unb zwanzigfte, &c.; 30th, ber breißigfte; 40th, ber vierzigfte; 50th, ber fünfzigfte; 60th, ber fechszigfte; 70th, ber fiebenzigfte; 80th, ber achtzigfte; 90th, ber neunzigfte; 100th, ber hundertfte; 101st, ber hundert unb erfte; 200th, ber zwei hundertfte; 1000th, ber taufenbfte.

Note 1.—The units always stand before the tens; but the last number only has the termination of the ordinal: ber zwei unb zwanzigfte.

Note 2.—The ordinal numbers admit the three forms of inflection of adjectives: erfter Aufzug, first act; ber erfte Aufzug, mein erfter Aufzug; gen. erftes Aufzuges, bes erften Aufzuges, meines erften Aufzuges, &c. &c.

Note 3.—The dimidiatives are expressed in the following strange manner: anberthalb, one and a half; brittehalb, two and a half; viertehalb, three and a half, &c.

They are indeclinable. The multiplicatives by einfach, zweifach, twofold, dreifach or zweifältig, dreifältig, &c. They are declined like adjectives. The variatives by einerlei, of one kind; zweierlei, dreierlei, &c. They are not declined. The fractionals by ein Drittel, a third; ein Viertel, ein Fünftel; they are substantives of the neuter gender. The reiteratives by einmal, once; zweimal, dreimal, or zwei Mal, drei Mal.

Note 4.— The indefinite numerals are (*a*) of number: jeder, jeglicher, jedweder, jedermann, every, every one, every body; mancher, many a one; mehrere, several; einige, etliche, some. They are all declined like adjectives, with the exception of jedermann, which is used as a substantive; only the genitive receives a mark of inflection, jedermanns. (*b*) Of quantity: etwas, some, something; nichts, nothing; ganz, whole; halb, half; etwas and nichts are never declined. Ganz and halb are declined like adjectives in the plural; and in the singular when preceded by an article or pronoun: ganze Tage, whole days; halbe Nächte, half the nights; das ganze Land, but ganz Deutschland. Also in the dative without any article or pronoun, but with a preposition: von ganzem Herzen, with the whole heart; (*c*) of number and quantity: all, aller, alle, alles, all; viel, much; wenig, little; mehr, more; genug, enough; kein, no, none; sämmtlich, or gesammt, all, whole; lauter, nothing but. Viel and wenig are declined like ganz and halb. Ein wenig, a little, remains entirely unaltered, unless it be used substantively. *Either* is expressed by einer, e, es, von beiden; *neither* by keiner, e, es, von beiden; *any body*, by jedermann; *any thing*, by alles; *any one*, irgend jemand; *any where*, irgend wo; *at any time*, zu irgend einer Zeit.

THE PRONOUNS.

1.—Personal, Reflective, and Reciprocal Pronouns.

	First Person.		Second Person.	
	Sing.	Plur.	Sing.	Plur.
N.	Ich, I.	Wir, we.	Du, thou.	Ihr, you.
G.	Meiner, of me.	Unſer, of us.	Deiner, of thee.	Euer, of you.
D.	Mir, to me.	Uns, to us.	Dir, to thee.	Euch, to you.
A.	Mich, me.	Uns, us.	Dich, thee.	Euch, you.

Third Person.

	Sing.			Plur.
	Masc.	*Fem.*	*Neut.*	
N.	Er, he.	Sie, her.	Es, it.	Sie, they.
G.	Seiner, of him.	Ihrer, of her.	Seiner, of it.	Ihrer, of them.
D.	Ihm, to him.	Ihr, to her.	Ihm, to it.	Ihnen, to them.
A.	Ihn, him.	Sie, her.	Es, it.	Sie.

Note.—The gen. cases, mein, dein, ſein, ihr, are absolute forms.

For the first and second person sing. and plur. the oblique cases of the personal pronouns are also used as reflective and reciprocal pronouns. For the third person there is a special reflective and reciprocal pronoun.

	Sing.		
	Masc.	*Fem.*	*Neut.*
N.	——	——	——
G.	Seiner, of himself.	Ihrer, of herself.	Seiner, of itself.
D.	Sich, to himself.	Sich, to herself.	Sich, to itself.
A.	Sich, himself.	Sich, herself.	Sich, itself.

Plur.

N.	——
G.	Ihrer, of themselves.
D.	Sich, to themselves.
A.	Sich, themselves.

Jd) liebe mid), I love myself; bu liebft bid), thou lovest thyself; er, fie, es liebt fid), he, she, it loves himself, herself, itself; wir lieben uns, we love ourselves, ihr liebt eud), you love yourselves; fie lieben fid), they love themselves (reflectives). Wir lieben uns, or, einanber, we love one another; ihr liebt eud), or, einanber, you love one another; fie lieben fid), or, einanber, they love one another.

Note 1.—Mark the difference of signification in myself, thyself, &c. I did it *myself*; this *myself* is not the reflective pronoun: id) that es felbft.

Note 2.—As the inanimate objects are either masc. fem. or neuter, the pronouns er, fie, es, must be used accordingly: Wo ift mein Huth? Er ift nid)t hier, id) habe ihn nid)t gefehen, where is my hat? It is not here, I have not seen it.

Note 3.—The neuter gender of the third personal pronoun es, is only used in the nominative and accusative, when it represents an inanimate object. For the other cases the demonstrative, beffen, bem, or beffelben, bemfelben, is used: er bietet mir Gelb an, aber id) bebarf beffen, or beffelben nid)t, he offers me money, but I am not in want of it.

Note 4.—The personal pronouns are seldom used with a preposition preceding, when they represent inanimate objects or abstract ideas; a demonstrative adverb which coalesces with the preposition, or the demonstrative pronoun, berfelbe, biefelbe, baffelbe, the same, is used: id) habe eine Bleifeber gefauft, aber id) fann bamit, or, mit berfelben nid)t fd)reiben, I have bought a pencil, but I cannot write with it. Damit is used for mit ihm, or ihr; baraus, for aus ihm or ihr; bavon, for von ihm or ihr; barauf, for auf ihn, fie, es, or ihm, ihr; barüber, for über ihn, es, &c. &c.

Note 5.—The Germans address those with whom they are not on intimate terms, or have not been acquainted

from their childhood, in the third person plural: Haben
Sie ihn gesehen? Have you seen him? Grown up persons
address children, children their parents, as well as each
other in the second person singular.   Haft Du ihn gesehen?
In writing, the pronoun of address must have a capital
initial.

The Possessive Pronouns.

These are

		Masc.	Fem.	Neut.
Sing.	1st pers.	mein.	meine.	mein, my.
	2d pers.	dein.	deine.	dein, thy.
	3d pers. masc.	fein.	feine.	fein, his.
	3d pers. fem.	ihr.	ihre.	ihr, her.
	3d pers. neut.	fein.	feine.	fein, its.
Plur.	1st pers.	unfer.	unfere.	unfer, our.
	2d pers.	euer.	euere.	euer, your.
	3d pers.	ihr.	ihre.	ihr, their.

Note 1.—In the sing. they are declined like the indefinite article; in the plur. like an adjective in the first
form of inflection.   When they stand before a substantive, the nominative sing. does not take the terminations
of the genders in the masc. and neuter: mein Vater; gen.
meines Vaters, unfer Kind; gen. unfers Kindes; dat. unferm
Kinde.

Note 2.—When they are used substantively, they
either receive the terminations of the genders, meiner,
meine, meines; or, are preceded by the definite article, and
declined like an adjective: der meine, die meine, das meine;
frequently the syllable ig is inserted, der meinige, die meinige,
das meinige, der unfrige, die unfrige, das unfrige.

Note 3.—The definite article is used instead of the
possessive pronouns, when the sense cannot be mistaken:

as, der Knabe hat einen Huth auf dem Kopfe, the boy has a hat on his head; it must be the boy's head.

Note 4.—The personal or reflective pronouns with an article before the substantive are used instead of the possessive, when not only possession is implied, but when the subject is affected, or a strong reference to the subject is expressed: ich habe es ihm in die Hand gegeben, I have given it into his hand; ich habe mir die Hand verwundet; I have wounded my hand; er hat sich den Hals abgeschnitten, he has cut his throat; das Herz klopft ihm vor Freude, his heart beats with joy.

The Demonstrative Pronouns.

They are
1. Dieser, diese, dieses, (cont. dies) this, Lat. *hic.*
2. Jener, jene, jenes, that, Lat. *ille.*
3. Der, die, das, that.
4. Derjenige, diejenige, dasjenige, that, Lat. *is.*
5. Derselbe, dieselbe, dasselbe, the same.
6. Solcher, solche, solches, such.

Dieser, diese, dieses, and jener, jene, jenes, are declined like an adjective in the first form of inflection. Derjenige, diejenige, dasjenige, and derselbe, dieselbe, dasselbe, are compounds; each component is declined, the former like the definite article, the latter like an adjective in the 2nd form of inflection; derjenige, diejenige, dasjenige, gen. desjenigen, derjenigen, desjenigen, plur. diejenigen, derjenigen, denjenigen, diejenigen. Solcher, solche, solches, is declined like an adjective. It is often preceded by the indefinite article, ein solcher Mann, eine solche Frau, ein solches Kind. It is also put before the article, and remains unaltered in all the cases; solch ein Mann, solch eine Frau, solch ein Kind. Der, die, das, is declined in the following manner:—

Sing.	Plur.
N. der, die, das.	N. die.
G. des, or der, or des, or	G. der derer, or deren.
dessen, deren, dessen.	
D. dem, der, dem.	D. den, or denen.
A. den, die, das.	A. die.

Note 1.—The demonstrative pronoun, *that*, has three different significations, as will be perceived in the following sentences. That tree which stands in that corner of my garden, is a good tree. I have bought the horse of my neighbour, and also that of his son. That tree which bears fruit, is a good tree. In each of these sentences, *that* must be expressed in German by a different pronoun.

Jener, jene, jenes, is used to point out a definite person or thing; as, jener Mann, welcher in jener Ecke steht, ist mein Freund, that man, who stands in that corner is my friend. Der, die, das, is used to avoid the repetition of a substantive. Ich bewundere Ihren Garten und auch den Ihres Sohnes, I admire your garden, and also that of your son. It is also used indefinitely; ich erinnere mich dessen nicht; I do not remember that; ich habe das nie gehört, I have never heard that. Derjenige, diejenige, dasjenige, is used to point out, or to distinguish indefinite persons, or things, and must be followed by the relative pronoun. That man who is cruel, cannot be good; derjenige Mensch, welcher grausam ist, kann nicht gut seyn. It can, however, not be denied, that der, die, das, is often used for, jener, jene, jenes, as well as for derjenige, diejenige, dasjenige. But the student should accustom himself to use the proper pronouns.

Note 2.—In English, the demonstrative pronouns are not used substantively, to point out persons; the personal pronouns are used instead; as, he who stands in that corner is my friend ; he who is contented is rich ; the happiness of him who fears God, is greater than the happiness of him who lives without God. In German, the demonstrative pronouns are used ; jener, to point out definite, derjenige, to point out indefinite persons.

Note 3.—The gen. deſſen, deren, is also employed instead of the possessive pronoun, when it refers to the object of the sentence, (like the Latin, *ejus*) to avoid ambiguity ; er malte ſeinen Vetter und deſſen Sohn, he painted his cousin, and his (the cousin's) son.

Note 4.—The adverbs hier, here, da, there, are used instead of demonstrative pronouns when connected with prepositions, and pointing out inanimate objects, or abstract ideas. Hier is used for dieſer, da for jener ; hier often loses r before a consonant ; da receives r before a vowel, and n ; as, hiermit, or hiemit, herewith ; for mit dieſem, hieraus, daraus, davon, hievon, damit, daburch, darnach, &c.

The Relative and Interrogative Pronouns.

These pronouns are either definite or indefinite. The definite is, welcher, welche, welches, who, and which, used of inanimate objects as well as of persons, and declined like an adjective in its first form of inflection. The indefinite is wer, who ; was, what. It is declined in the following manner ; but it is so indefinite, that it has neither feminine gender, nor plural number :

N.	wer, who	was, what.
G.	weſſen, whose	weſſen.
D.	wem, to whom	wem.
A.	wen, whom	was.

Note 1.—The definite pronoun must be used in reference to a particular person or thing, or to a particular

D

word; as, the man who sold me the horse, is dead; the horse, which I bought, is good; he, who stands there, is my son; which of your brothers is gone to Germany? The indefinite pronoun must be used in reference to an indefinite person, or thing; as, I cannot tell you who recommended me the book; we do not know, whose house it is; who was there? what did he say? It is always used after the neuter of the indefinite numerals, alles, etwas, manches, nichts, viel, wenig; as, alles, was ich habe, all that I have.

Note 2.—The demonstrative, der, die, das, is *frequently* used for the relative, welcher, welche, welches; and always, after the 1st and 2nd personal pronouns, when these pronouns are repeated; as, ich, der ich, I, who; du, der du, thou, who; wir, die wir, we, who; ihr, die ihr, you, who; also after the pronoun of address; Sie, die sie, you who. In this case, the verb must agree with the pronoun; du, der du es mir sagtest. This pronoun is likewise preferred, when the genitive of the relative is required; and this genitive never stands after the substantive, by which it is governed; as, the man, whose house I saw, der Mann, dessen Haus ich sah; the woman whose child is ill, die Frau, deren Kind krank ist; charity, the practice of which is commanded, is a noble virtue, die Liebe, deren Uebung geboten ist, ist eine edle Tugend.

Note 3.—Was für, either with or without the indefinite article, expresses species or quality (Latin, *qualis*): was für ein Mann; what kind of man; was für Wein, what sort of wine. Was and für are sometimes separated.

Note 4.—The adverb *ever*, after these pronouns, is expressed by auch, or immer.

Note 5.—The adverb wo is, like the demonstrative da, used with prepositions; and r is inserted when the preposition begins with a vowel; woburd), worin, woraus, worüber, &c. &c.

Note 6.—The relative pronoun is never omitted in German. The book you love, das Buch, welches Sie lieben.

The Indefinite Pronouns.

These are: einer, e, es, one, some one; keiner, e, es, no one; jemand, somebody, any body; niemand, nobody; etwas, something, anything; nichts, nothing; and, man, one, (French *on*.)

Jemand and niemand take es in the genitive; in the dative, they either remain unaltered, or take en; the accusative is like the nominative. The oblique cases of man are formed of einer; man kann nicht immer erhalten, was einem gefällt, one cannot always get, what pleases one.

Selbst or selber has two significations; 1. self, ich selbst, I myself; 2. even, selbst sein Vater wußte es nicht, even his father did not know it. It is not declined.

THE VERBS.
Preliminary Remarks.

1. The principal parts of the verb in the active voice are: 1, The Infinitive Mood; 2, The Present Tense: 3, The Imperfect; and 4, The Preterite Participle. If the verb be regular, the formation of these parts is very simple. From the infinitive mood, which always ends in en: lieben, *to love*, the first person of the present tense is formed by dropping the n: ich liebe, I love; from the present, the imperfect is formed by adding te: ich liebete (con. liebte); and from the imperfect, the participle, by dropping the final e, and putting the augment ge before it: geliebt. From these parts all other tenses and moods are formed.

2. The terminations of the persons of the present and imperfect, are as follows:—

Present.		Imperfect.	
IND.	SUBJ.	IND.	SUBJ.
Sing.		**Sing.**	
1 e.	1 e.	1 ete, or te.	1 ete.
2 eſt, or ſt.	2 eſt.	2 eteſt, or teſt.	2 eteſt.
3 et, or t.	3 e.	3 ete, or te.	3 ete.
Plur.		**Plur.**	
1 en.	1 en.	1 eten, or ten.	1 eten.
2 et, or t.	2 et.	2 etet, or tet.	2 etet.
3 en.	3 en.	3 eten, or ten.	3 eten.

IMPERATIVE.	INFINITIVE.	PARTICIPLES.
Sing.		
2 e.	en.	*Pres.* enb.
3 e.		*Pret.* et, or t.
Plur.		
1 en.		
2 et, or t.		
3 en.		

Note.—The *e* before the ſt or *t* of the ind. and imp. moods, and the pret. part., is generally omitted if the word can be pronounced without difficulty: as, liebte.

3. The perfect, pluperf. and future tenses are formed by means of auxiliary verbs.

4. In the German language, there is no special form for that tense which, in the Greek Verb, is called the Aorist, a tense which is used to express a past action or event without any relation to another, and without representing that action or event, as still existing in its consequences. In German, as in Latin, the perfect is used instead.

5. Besides the above-mentioned moods, the ind., the subj., the imp., and the inf., there is a conditional mood of the present, the perfect, the first and second future.

That of the present and perfect is, *in form*, the subj.
mood of the imperf. and pluperf. and that of the future is
formed by the subj. mood of the third auxiliary, as will
be apparent from the paradigm of the verb; but no notice
will here be taken of the conditional mood of the present
and perfect.

6. A supine is formed by putting the preposition ju
before the inf. ; and a future participle, by putting that
preposition before the present participle : ju lieben, ju
liebend, of praising, to be praised.

7. The whole of the passive Voice is formed by means
of an auxiliary Verb.

Note.—The form of the verb in the 3rd person sing.
being the same for the masc., fem., and neut., the pronouns for the fem. and neut. will be omitted in all
paradigms, to avoid the unnecessary repetition of er, sie, es.

AUXILIARY VERBS OF TENSES.

Auxiliary verbs of tenses are those which are used for
the formation of certain tenses, and without which no
complete conjugation can be formed. There are three
in German : (*a*) haben, to have ; (*b*) seyn, to be ; (*c*)
werden, to become. They are all irregular.

(a) Haben, TO HAVE.

Principal parts : Haben, habe, hatte, gehabt.

PRESENT.

Indicative.	*Subjunctive.*
Ich habe, I have.	Ich habe, I may have.
Du hast, thou hast.	Du habest, thou mayst have.
Er hat, he has.	Er habe, he may have.
Wir haben, we have.	Wir haben, we may have.
Ihr habt, ye have.	Ihr habet, ye may have,
Sie haben, they have.	Sie haben, they may have.

D 3

Indict.   *Subjunct.*

IMPERFECT.

Ich hatte, I had.	Ich hätte, I might have.
Du hattest, thou hadst.	Du hättest, thou mightst have.
Er hatte, he had.	Er hätte, he might have.
Wir hatten, we had.	Wir hätten, we might have.
Ihr hattet, ye had.	Ihr hättet, ye might have.
Sie hatten, they had.	Sie hätten, they might have.

PERFECT.

Ich habe gehabt, I have had.	Ich habe gehabt, I may have had.
Du hast gehabt, thou hast had, &c. &c.	Du habest gehabt, thou mayst have had, &c. &c.

PLUPERFECT.

Ich hatte gehabt, I had had.	Ich hätte gehabt, I might have had.
Du hattest gehabt, thou hadst had.	Du hättest gehabt, thou mightst have had.

FIRST FUTURE.

Ich werde haben, I shall have.	Ich werde haben, I shall have.
Du wirst haben, thou wilt have.	Du werdest haben, &c.
Er wird haben, he will have.	Er werde haben, &c.
Wir werden haben, we shall have.	Wir werden haben, &c.
Ihr werdet haben, ye will have.	Ihr werdet haben, &c.
Sie werden haben, they will have.	Sie werden haben, &c.

SECOND FUTURE.

Ich werde gehabt haben, I shall have had.	Ich werde gehabt haben, I shall have had.
Du wirst gehabt haben, thou wilt have had. &c.	Du werdest gehabt haben, thou wilt have had. &c.

Indicative.   *Subjunctive.*

FIRST CONDITIONAL.

Jch würde haben, I should have.
Du würdeſt haben, thou wouldst have.
Er würde haben, he would have.
Wir würden haben, we should have.
Ihr würdet haben, ye would have.
Sie würden haben, they would have.

SECOND CONDITIONAL.

Jch würde gehabt haben, I should have had.
Du würdeſt gehabt haben, thou wouldst have had.

IMPERATIVE.

Habe (du), have (thou).   Haben wir, let us have.
Habe er, let him have.   Habt (ihr), have (ye).
                            Haben ſie, let them have.

INFINITIVE.

Pres.   Haben, to have.
Perf.   Gehabt haben, to have had.
Fut.   Haben werden, to be about to have.

PARTICIPLES.

Pres. Habend, having.   *Pret.* Gehabt, had.

Note.—Instead of the 1st pers. plur., of the imp. mood, the auxiliary verb of mood, laſſen, with the infinitive is most frequently employed: lieben wir, is expressed either by laß uns lieben, or laßt uns lieben, or laſſen Sie uns lieben, according to the different way of address.

(b.) Seyn, TO BE.

The principal parts of this auxiliary verb are derived from different roots, and are therefore quite irregular. Seyn, bin, war, geweſen.

Indicative.	*Subjunctive.*

PRESENT.

Ich bin, I am.	Ich sey, I may be.
Du bist, thou art.	Du seyest (seyst), thou mayst be.
Er ist, he is.	Er sey, he may be.
Wir sind, we are.	Wir seyen (seyn), we may be.
Ihr seyd, ye are.	Ihr seyet, ye may be.
Sie sind, they are.	Sie seyen (seyn), they may be.

IMPERFECT.

Ich war, I was.	Ich wäre, I might be.
Du warest (warst), thou wast.	Du wärest (wärst), thou, &c.
Er war, he was.	Er wäre, he might be.
Wir waren, we were.	Wir wären, we might be.
Ihr waret, (wart), ye were.	Ihr wäret (wärt), ye might be.
Sie waren, they were.	Sie wären, they might be.

PERFECT.

Ich bin gewesen, I have been.	Ich sey gewesen, I may have been.
Du bist gewesen, thou hast been. &c.	Du seyst gewesen, thou mayst have been. &c.

PLUPERFECT.

Ich war gewesen, I had been.	Ich wäre gewesen, I might have been.
Du warest (warst) gewesen, thou hadst been, &c.	Du wärest (wärst) gewesen, thou mightst have been. &c.

FIRST FUTURE.

Ich werde seyn, I shall be.	Ich werde seyn, I shall be.
Du wirst seyn, thou wilt be, &c.	Du werdest seyn, thou wilt be, &c.

SECOND FUTURE.

Ich werde gewesen seyn, I shall have been.	Ich werde gewesen seyn, I shall have been.
Du wirst gewesen seyn, thou wilt have been. &c.	Du werdest gewesen seyn, thou wilt have been. &c.

FIRST CONDITIONAL.

Ich wůrde ſeyn, I should be.

Du wårdeſt ſeyn, thou wouldst be. &c.

SECOND CONDITIONAL.

Ich wůrde geweſen ſeyn, I should have been.

Du wůrdeſt geweſen ſeyn, thou wouldst have been, &c.

IMPERATIVE.

Sey (du), be thou.　　　　Seyn wir, let us be.

Sey er, let him be.　　　　Seyb (ihr), be ye.

　　　　　　　　　　　　Seyn ſie, let them be.

INFINITIVE.

Pres. Seyn, to be.

Perf. Geweſen ſeyn, to have been.

Fut. Seyn werden, to be about to be.

PARTICIPLES.

Pres. Seyend, being.　　　*Pret.* Geweſen, being.

(o) Werden, TO BECOME.

Principal parts: Werden, werde, wurde, geworden.

This auxiliary verb has a special form for the sing. of the aorist: ich ward, du wardſt, er ward; but as no other verb has this peculiarity, it may be dispensed with; most authors always use wurde. The pret. participle is geworden, when it is used as a notional verb, but worden when employed as an auxiliary verb, to avoid the re-occurrence of the augment ge.

　　Indicative.　　　　　　　*Subjunctive.*

PRESENT.

Ich werde, I become.　　　　Ich werde, I may become.

Du wirſt, thou becomest.　　Du werdeſt, thou mayst become.

Er wird, he becomes.　　　　Er werde, he may become.

Indict.	*Subjunct.*
Wir werden, we become.	Wir werden, we may become.
Ihr werbet, ye become.	Ihr werbet, ye may become.
Sie werden, they become.	Sie werden, they may become.

IMPERFECT.

Ich wurbe, I became.	Ich würbe, I might become.
Du wurbest, thou becamest.	Du würbest, thou mightst, &c.
Er wurbe, he became.	Er würbe, he might become.
Wir wurben, we became.	Wir würben, we might become.
Ihr wurbet, ye became.	Ihr würbet, ye might become.
Sie wurben, they became.	Sie würben, they might become.

PERFECT.

Ich bin geworben, I have become, &c.	Ich sey geworben, I may have become, &c.

PLUPERFECT.

Ich war geworben, I had become, &c.	Ich wäre geworben, I might have become, &c.

FIRST FUTURE.

Ich werbe werden, I shall become, &c.	Ich werbe werden, I shall become, &c.

SECOND FUTURE.

Ich werbe geworben seyn, I shall have become, &c.	Ich werbe geworben seyn, I shall have become, &c.

FIRST CONDITIONAL.

Ich würbe werden, I should become, &c.

SECOND CONDITIONAL.

Ich würbe geworben seyn, I should have become.

IMPERATIVE.

werbe (bu), become (thou).	werben wir, let us become.
werbe er, let him become.	werbet (ihr), become ye.
	werben sie, let them become.

INFINITIVE.

Pres. werben, to become.

Perf. geworben ſeyn, to have become.

Fut. werben werben, to be about to become.

PARTICIPLES.

Pres. werbenb, becoming.

Pret. geworben, become.

THE CONJUGATION OF THE REGULAR VERB.

(a) *Active Voice.*

Lieben, TO LOVE.

Principal parts :—Lieben, liebe, liebte, geliebt.

Indicative.	*Subjunctive.*
PRÈSENT.	
Ich liebe, I love.	Ich liebe, I may love.
Du liebeſt (liebſt), thou lovest.	Du liebeſt, thou mayst love.
Er liebt, he loves.	Er liebe, he may love.
Wir lieben, we love.	Wir lieben, we may love.
Ihr liebet (liebt), ye love.	Ihr liebet, ye may love.
Sie lieben, they love.	Sie lieben, they may love.
IMPERFECT.	
Ich liebte, I loved.	Ich liebete, I might love.
Du liebteſt, thou lovedst.	Du liebeteſt, thou mightst love.
Er liebte, he loved.	Er liebete, he might love.
Wir liebten, we loved.	Wir liebeten, we might love.
Ihr liebtet, ye loved.	Ihr liebetet, ye might love.
Sie liebten, they loved.	Sie liebeten, they might love.
PERFECT.	
Ich habe geliebt, I have loved, &c.	Ich habe geliebt, I may have loved, &c.

Indicative. *Subjunctive.*

PLUPERFECT.

Ich hatte geliebt, I had loved, &c.   Ich hätte geliebt, I might have loved, &c.

FIRST FUTURE.

Ich werde lieben, I shall love, &c.   Ich werde lieben, I shall love, &c.

SECOND FUTURE.

Ich werde geliebt haben, I shall have loved, &c.   Ich werde geliebt haben, I shall have loved, &c.

FIRST CONDITIONAL.

Ich würde lieben, I should love.

SECOND CONDITIONAL.

Ich würde geliebt haben, I should have loved.

IMPERATIVE.

Liebe (du), love (thou).   Lieben wir, let us love.
Liebe er, let him love.   Liebet (ihr), love ye.
Lieben sie, let them love.

INFINITIVE.

Pres. Lieben, to love.
Perf. Geliebt haben, to have loved.
Fut. Lieben werden, to be about to love.

PARTICIPLES.

Pres. Liebend, loving.   *Pret.* Geliebt, loved.

Observations.

1. In those verbs which have l or r for their final radical consonant, the e of the termination en is always left out in prose: as, sammeln for sammelen, to gather; dauern for daueren, to last; also frequently after h: as, blüh'n for blühen, to bloom; seh'n for sehen, to see: geh'n

for geßen, to go; but in the latter case, an apostrophe ought to be put instead of the *e*. When the l or r of the above-mentioned verbs is followed by *e* only as the characteristic termination of the person, the *e* of the root is left out: as, ich ſammle for ſammele; ich baure for bauere.

2. Verbs of foreign origin ending in iren or ieren, and some German verbs formed by the termination ieren, do not take the augment ge in the pret. participle: bociren, to teach; ſtubiren, to study; circuliren, to circulate; marſchiren, to march; buchſtabiren, to spell; regieren, to reign; ſpazieren, to walk; barbieren, to shave; part. bocirt, ſtubirt, &c. But some true German verbs as zieren, to adorn; frieren, to freeze, must not be confounded with them. The augment is also omitted, when the infinitive has the *prefix*. ge: as, geloben, par. gelobt.

(b) *Passive Voice.*

PRESENT.

Indicative.	*Subjunctive.*
Ich werbe geliebt, I am loved, &c.	Ich werbe geliebt, I may be loved, &c.

IMPERFECT.

Ich wurbe geliebt, I was loved.	Ich würbe geliebt, I might be loved.

PERFECT.

Ich bin geliebt worben, I have been loved.	Ich ſey geliebt worben, I may have been loved.

PLUPERFECT.

Ich war geliebt worben, I had been loved.	Ich wäre geliebt worben, I might have been loved.

FIRST FUTURE.

Ich werbe geliebt werben, I shall be loved.	Ich werbe geliebt werben, I shall be loved.

E

SECOND FUTURE.

Ich werbe geliebt worben seyn, I   Ich werbe geliebt worben seyn,
shall have been loved.   I shall have been loved.

FIRST CONDITIONAL.

Ich würbe geliebt werben, I should be loved.

SECOND CONDITIONAL.

Ich würbe geliebt worben seyn, I should have been loved.

IMPERATIVE.

Werbe (bu) geliebt, be (thou)   Werben wir geliebt, let us be
  loved.   loved.

Werbe er geliebt, let him be   Werbet (ihr) geliebt, be (ye)
  loved.   loved.

                                Werben sie geliebt, let them be
                                  loved.

INFINITIVE.

Pres. Geliebt werben, to be loved.

Perf. Geliebt worben seyn, to have been loved.

Fut. Werben geliebt werben, to be about to be loved.

PARTICIPLE.
Geliebt, loved.

Note 1.—The participle geliebt belongs to the active as
well as to the passive voice.

Note 2.—The participle of the auxiliary worben is, in
the perf. and pluperf., sometimes left out; but it is more
correct to use it.

AUXILIARY VERBS OF MOODS.

Auxiliary Verbs of Moods are those which convey no
idea in themselves, but give a certain modification to a
notional verb by expressing the *possibility* or *necessity*,
the *lawfulness* or *willingness*, of what is indicated by that
verb. They are: ich mag, I may; ich will, I will; ich soll,
I shall; ich kann, I can; ich barf, I dare; ich muß, I must;

ich laſſe, I let. They require the verb, which they modify in the infinitive; and when the participle of the compound tenses is preceded by such an infinitive, it is changed into the infinitive: ich hätte ihn ſehen können (not gekonnt), I might have seen him. All of them are irregular; and as a perfect acquaintance with them is of great importance, I shall first state the conjugation of each, and then add some observations on the use and signification of them.

1. Ich mag, I may; inf. mögen.

Pres. Ind.	Ich mag.	*Subj.*	Ich möge.
	Du magſt.		Du mögeſt.
	Er mag.		Er möge.
	Wir mögen.		Wir mögen.
	Ihr möget (or mögt).		Ihr möget.
	Sie mögen.		Sie mögen.

Imperf. Ind.	Ich mochte.	*Subj.*	Ich möchte.
Perf.	Ich habe gemocht.		Ich habe gemocht.
Plup.	Ich hatte gemocht.		Ich hätte gemocht.
1st Fut.	Ich werde mögen.		Ich werde mögen.
2nd Fut.	Ich werde gemocht haben.		Ich werde gemocht haben.

1st Conditional. Ich würde mögen.

2nd ———— Ich würde gemocht haben.

Obs.—Mögen signifies:—1. *To be permitted, to be at liberty;* but differs from dürfen, to be allowed: er mag lachen means, he may laugh; no objection is made to his laughing; er darf lachen means, nobody can forbid him to laugh.—2. *Chance* or *possibility;* especially in the subj. of the imperf.: es möchte regnen, it might rain; er möchte kommen, he might come. In the subj. mood of that tense it expresses also an *inclination:* ich möchte es bezweifeln, I am inclined to doubt it.—3. *A wish, desire;* especially in the subj. of the present and imperfect: möge er lange leben, may he live long; möge es der Himmel geben, may

Heaven grant it; idh möchte wohl etwas davon haben, I should like to have some of it.—4. *To like :* idh mag es nidht thun, I do not like to do it; idh habe es nidht thun mögen (not gemodht), I have not liked to do it. In this significa-tion it is often applied to what is eaten or drunk, without an infinitive : idh mag biefen Wein nidht, I do not like this wine; idh habe ihn nie gemodht (not mögen), I have never liked it.

2.—Ich will, I will; inf. wollen.

Pres. Ind.	Ich will.	Subj.	Ich wolle.
	Du willft.		Du wolleft.
	Er will.		Er wolle.
	Wir wollen.		Wir wollen.
	Ihr wollet (wollt).		Ihr wollet.
	Sie wollen.		Sie wollen.
Imperf.	Ich wollte.		Ich wollte.
Perf.	Ich habe gewollt.		Ich habe gewollt.
Pluperf.	Ich hatte gewollt.		Ich hätte gewollt.
1st Fut.	Ich werbe wollen.		Ich werbe wollen.
2nd Fut.	Ich werbe gewollt haben.		Ich werbe gewollt haben.

1st *Conditional.* Ich würbe wollen.

2nd ————— Ich würbe gewollt haben.

Obs.—This auxiliary is never used to denote future time, not being an auxiliary verb of tenses. It expresses : —1. *Will, intention, inclination :* idh will lefen, I will read; er will gehen, he will go; idh habe fpielen wollen (not gewollt), I have wished to play; idh wollte, bu könnteft jezt kommen, I wish thou couldst come now.—2. It sometimes conveys the meaning, *to maintain, assert :* er will ben Kometen, welcher erwartet wirb, fdhon gefehen haben, he main-tains that he has seen already the comet which is expected (like the Latin *velle ;* see Virg. Æn. i. 630).—3. It is used to express a command in strong terms: wollt ihr vom Platz, be gone; willſt du ſtille ſeyn, be quiet.

3. Ich ſoll, I shall; inf. ſollen.

Pres. Ind.	Ich ſoll.	*Subj.*	Ich ſolle.
	Du ſollſt.		Du ſolleſt.
	Er ſoll.		Er ſolle.
	Wir ſollen.		Wir ſollen.
	Ihr ſollet (ſollt).		Ihr ſollet.
	Sie ſollen.		Sie ſollen.
Imperf.	Ich ſollte.		Ich ſollte.
Perf.	Ich habe geſollt.		Ich habe geſollt.
Pluperf.	Ich hatte geſollt.		Ich hätte geſollt.
1st Fut.	Ich werde ſollen.		Ich werde ſollen.
2nd Fut.	Ich werde geſollt haben.		Ich werde geſollt haben.

1st Conditional. Ich würde ſollen.

2nd ———— Ich würde geſollt haben.

Obs.—Sollen signifies:—1. To be obliged by *moral* necessity, enforced by the command of another: ich ſollte es thun, I ought to do it; du ſollſt Gott, deinen Herrn, lieben von ganzem Herzen, thou shalt love God, thy Lord, with thy whole heart; er ſoll gehen, he is to go; er hätte es thun ſollen (not geſollt), he ought to have done it.—2. To be admitted, to be supposed; du ſollſt mich nicht beleidigt haben, I admit that thou didst not offend me.—3. To be said, reported; Latin, *dici:* das Parlament ſoll ſich am 10ten dieſes Monats verſammeln, it is said Parliament will assemble on the 10th of this month; dieſer Umſtand ſoll ſich nie zugetragen haben, it is said that this circumstance never occurred.—4. The imperfect is used to express:— (*a*) a condition of a *definite* act or event: wenn er kommen ſollte, ſo will ich es ihm ſagen, if he should come, I will tell him so; ſollte das Wetter ſich ändern, ſo werde ich ausgehen, should the weather change, I shall go out:—(*b*) a ques-

E 3

tion implying either surprise or doubt : follte bas wahr
feyn? can that be true?—5. Sollen is often used eliptically, an infinitive being understood; (a) thun, to do;
was foll ich, what am I to do? what am I wanted for?
(b) heißen, to mean: was foll bas, what is the meaning of
that? was foll biefe Rebe? was follen biefe Thränen? (c)
bienen, to serve: wozu foll biefe Klage? what purpose does
this complaint serve? was foll mir ein eitler Titel? of what
use is a vain title to me?

4. Ich kann, I can; inf. können.

Pres. Ind.		Subj.	
	Ich kann.		Ich könne.
	Du kannst.		Du könnest.
	Er kann.		Er könne.
	Wir können.		Wir können.
	Ihr könnet (könnt).		Ihr könnet.
	Sie können.		Sie können,
Imperf.	Ich konnte.		Ich könnte.
Perf.	Ich habe gekonnt.		Ich habe gekonnt.
Pluperf.	Ich hatte gekonnt.		Ich hätte gekonnt.
1st Fut.	Ich werde können.		Ich werde können.
2nd Fut.	Ich werde gekonnt haben.		Ich werde gekonnt haben.

1st *Conditional.* Ich würde können.

2nd ———— Ich würde gekonnt haben.

Obs.—Können denotes :—1. Physical and moral possibility: ich kann lefen und fchreiben, I can read and write;
ich habe heute nicht fchreiben können (not gekonnt), I have not
been able to write to-day; er kann jetzt wieder gehen, he can
now walk again; du kannst ausgehen, wenn du willft, thou
mayst go out if thou likest; er kann es verftanden haben,
he may have understood it; this differs from er hat es
verftehen können, he has been able to understand it.—
2. The subj. mood of the imperf. and plup. is used to
make an expression more polite: Sie könnten mir das

Buch wohl geben, you might, indeed, give me the book; du hätteſt es mir wohl ſagen können, thou mightst, indeed, have informed me of it.—3. It is used eliptically, an infinitive being understood: (a) thun, to do; wir können nicht immer, was wir wollen, we cannot always do what we wish (like the Scotch *can*); (b) ſagen, to say; der Knabe hat ſeine Aufgabe nicht gekonnt (not können), the boy has not been able to say his lesson; (c) leſen, ſprechen, verſtehen, to read, speak, understand; er kann Deutſch, he knows German.

5. Ich darf, I dare; inf. dürfen.

Pres. Ind.	Ich darf.	*Subj.*	Ich dürfe.
	Du darfſt.		Du dürfeſt.
	Er darf.		Er dürfe.
	Wir dürfen.		Wir dürfen.
	Ihr dürfet (dürſt).		Ihr dürfet.
	Sie dürfen.		Sie dürfen.
Imperf.	Ich durfte.		Ich dürfte.
Perf.	Ich habe gedurft.		Ich habe gedurft.
Plup.	Ich hatte gedurft.		Ich hätte gedurft.
1*st Fut.*	Ich werde dürfen.		Ich werde dürfen.
2*nd Fut.*	Ich werde gedurft haben.		Ich werde gedurft haben.

1*st Conditional.* Ich würde dürfen.

2*nd* ————— Ich würde gedurft haben.

Obs.— Dürfen signifies :—1. To dare, to venture; ich darf ihm die Wahrheit ſagen, I venture to speak the truth to him.—2. To be allowed, not to be restrained: darf ich fragen? may I ask? (this differs from mag ich fragen? see mögen); Sie dürfen es wiſſen, you may know it (Sie mögen es wiſſen); ich habe es nicht thun dürfen (not gedurft), I have not been allowed to do it. With the negative it is to be rendered by *may not, must not, dare not:* ich darf heute nicht ausgehen, denn ich habe mich erkältet, I must not

go out to-day, for I have taken cold.—3. The subj. mood
of the imperf. denotes a probable contingency, and may
be translated by *might, may, need, should, would:* es
dürfte vielleicht wahr seyn, it might, perhaps, be true.

6. Ich muß, I must; inf. müssen.

Pres. Ind.	Ich muß.	Subj.	Ich müsse.
	Du mußt.		Du müssest.
	Er muß.		Er müsse.
	Wir müssen.		Wir müssen.
	Ihr müsset (müßt).		Ihr müsset.
	Sie müssen.		Sie müssen.
Imperf.	Ich mußte.		Ich müßte.
Perf.	Ich habe gemußt.		Ich habe gemußt.
Pluperf.	Ich hatte gemußt.		Ich hätte gemußt.
1st Fut.	Ich werde müssen.		Ich werde müssen.
2nd Fut.	Ich werde gemußt haben.		Ich werde gemußt haben.

1st *Conditional.* Ich würde müssen.

2nd ————— Ich würde gemußt haben.

Obs.—Müssen has nearly the same signification as the
English *must:* wir müssen alle offenbart werden vor dem
Richterstuhl Christi (2 Cor. v. 10); ein jeder Unterthan muß
den Gesetzen des Landes gehorchen, every subject must obey
the laws of the land; er muß ein reicher Mann seyn, he must
be a rich man; ich muß meinen Freund vertheidigen, I must
defend my friend; muß ich es thun? must I do it? It is
also used eliptically, an infinitive being understoood:
ich muß heute noch zurück (i. e. gehen), I must return to-
day.

7. Ich lasse, I let; inf. lassen.

Pres. Ind.	Ich lasse.	Subj.	Ich lasse.
	Du lässest.		Du lassest.
	Er läßt.		Er lasse.
	Wir lassen.		Wir lassen.
	Ihr lasset (laßt).		Ihr lasset.
	Sie lassen.		Sie lassen.

Imperf.	Ich ließ.	Ich ließe.
Perf.	Ich habe gelassen.	Ich habe gelassen.
Pluperf.	Ich hatte gelassen.	Ich hätte gelassen.
1st Fut.	Ich werde lassen.	Ich werde lassen.
2nd Fut.	Ich werde gelassen haben.	Ich werde gelassen haben.

1st Conditional. Ich würde lassen.

2nd ———— Ich würde gelassen haben.

Imperat. Laß.

Obs.—Lassen signifies :—1. To let, to suffer; ich lasse ihn gehen, I let him go; ich habe ihn gehen lassen (not gelassen), I have suffered him to go.—2. to make; laß ihn doch hinausgehen, pray, make him go out.—3. To leave ; das lasse ich bleiben, I leave that alone.—4. To let go; ich lasse dich nicht, du segnest mich denn; Gen. xxxii. 26.—5. To cause, to get, to order, always with the infinitive of the active, although the signification be passive: ich habe meinen Schuhmacher kommen lassen, I have ordered my shoe-maker to come ; der König hat den Verbrecher hinrichten lassen, the king has ordered the criminal to be executed; ich habe mir ein Paar Schuhe machen lassen, I have had a pair of shoes made for me.—6. With the reflective pronoun for the third person, sich, it is to be rendered by *may, is to be* : das läßt sich nicht thun, that is not to be done ; davon ließe sich vieles sagen, of that much might be said ; das läßt sich nicht begreifen, that is not to be comprehended.

IRREGULAR VERBS.

Those verbs are called irregular, which deviate from the formation and conjugation of lieben. This deviation takes place in a large number of verbs in the imperfect and the preterite participle; in several also in the present tense, especially in the second and third persons, and in the imperative mood.

The irregular verbs may be divided into two classes :
1. such as have the regular terminations of the imperfect
and participle, but change the radical vowel : as, nennen,
to name, imp. nannte, part. genannt :—2. such as have not
the termination te in the imperfect, and make the participle to end in en : as singen, to sing. imperf. sang, part.
gesungen.

The first class comprises only a small number ; bringen,
to bring ; brennen, to burn ; denken, to think ; kennen, to
know ; nennen, to name ; rennen, to run ; senden, to send ;
wenden, to turn ; and these change the radical vowel in
the imperfect and participle into a : as, brennen, brannte,
gebrannt. Bringen and denken change also the g and k
into ch, and throw out the n : bringen, brachte, gebracht ;
denken, dachte, gedacht.

The second class may be subdivided into three kinds :
—1. such as have three different vowels or diphthongs in
the present, imperf. and the participle :—2. such as have
the same vowel or diphthong in the imperfect and participle, but a different one from the present ;—3. such as
have the same vowel or diphthong in the present and participle, but a different one from the imperfect.

Infinitive.	Imperfect.	Participle.
1. Singen, to sing,	sang,	gesungen.
Nehmen, to take,	nahm,	genommen.
Bitten, to beg,	bat,	gebeten.
Gehen, to go,	ging,	gegangen.
2. Bieten, to offer,	bot,	geboten.
Heben, to lift,	hob,	gehoben.
Leiden, to suffer,	litt,	gelitten.
Meiden, to avoid,	mied,	gemieden.
3. Kommen, to come,	kam,	gekommen.
Laufen, to run,	lief,	gelaufen.
Rufen, to call,	rief,	gerufen.
Tragen, to carry,	trug,	getragen.

Those which have —

a in the 1st pers. pres. take á in the 2nd and 3rd sing.

e (long) ———————— ie ——————

e˙ (short) ———————— i ——————

and such as have t or th, for their last radical consonant do not take an additional syllable in the 3rd pers. sing. as, ſchelten, not er ſchietet, but er ſchilt; rathen, not er ráthet, but er ráth.

Examples, a : ich fange, I catch ; du fángſt, er fángt. *Exc.* ſchaffen, to create ; mahlen, to grind ; ſchallen (erſchallen), to sound :—e (long) : ich leſe, I read ; du lieſeſt, er lieſet. *Exc.* nehmen, to take, and treten, to tread, take a short i : du nimmſt, er nimmt; du trittſt, er tritt; and bewegen, to induce ; geneſen, to recover ; heben, to lift, form the pres. regularly :—e (short) : ich helfe, I help ; du hilfſt, er hilft. *Exc.* gehen, to go ; ſtehen, to stand.

Ich löſche, I extinguish, has,—du liſcheſt, er liſcht ; ich ſtoße, I push ; du ſtößeſt, er ſtößt, and ich komme, I come, either du kömmſt, er kömmt, or, which is more usual, du kommſt, er kommt.

All those which change the e of the 1st pers. present into ie or i in the 2nd and 3rd, take the same letters in the 2nd pers. of the imper. mood, and drop the characteristic final e : lies, read ; hilf, help. The 3rd pers. sing. and the whole of the plur. of the imperat. are formed regularly : leſe er, let him read ; leſet ihr, read ye. Of all other verbs the imper. is regular ; the unaccented e of the termination is sometimes omitted.

The subj. mood of the imperf. is formed by changing a, o, u, into á, ö, ü, and those which have no termination of the tense in the ind. take e in the subj. : ich bringe, I bring ; brachte, bráchte ; Ich denke, I think, dachte, báchte ; ich bitte, I beg, bat, báte ; ich hebe, I lift, hob, höbe ; ich ſinge, I sing, ſang, ſánge ; ich laufe, I run, lief, liefe. The following verbs, however,—nennen, to name; fennen, to know; rennen, to run; brennen, to burn; wenden, to turn; senden, to send,—form the subj. mood of the imperf., as if the verb were regular: ich nenne, imp. ind. nannte, subj. nennete; ich sende, I send, imp. ind. sandte, subj. sendete.

Some had formerly not those vowels in the imperf. which now occur in that tense, though they are still irregular. Of these verbs the subjunctive mood of the imperf. is formed from the antiquated tense, by changing a, o, u, into ā, ö, ū.

	Imperf.	Antiq.	Subj.
befehlen, to command,	befahl	befohl	befōhle
beginnen, to begin,	begann	begonn	begönne
bergen, to hide,	barg	burg	bürge
gebären, to bring forth,	gebar	gebor	gebōre
gelten, to be worth,	galt	golt	gölte
rinnen, to run, flow,	rann	ronn	rönne
spinnen, to spin,	spann	sponn	spönne
stehlen, to steal,	stahl	stohl	stöhle
sterben, to die,	starb	sturb	stürbe
verderben, to be spoiled,	verdarb	verdurb	verdürbe

Those verbs which have ie or ū for their radical vowel, formerly changed these vowels frequently into eu in the 2nd and 3rd pers. sing. of the pres. and 2nd sing. of the imperat., which is still the case in poetry: bieten, to offer; beutst, bent (not beutet), fließen, to flow, fleußt (Exod. iii. 8.), imper. fleuß; ziehen, to draw, imper. zeuch; trügen, to deceive, treugt; lügen, to lie; leugt, &c.

The verb essen, to eat, formerly dropped the e of the augment: gessen instead of geessen; but now g is inserted between the two e's: gegessen. Wissen, to know, is, like the auxiliary verbs of moods, irregular in the sing. of the pres.: ich weiß, du weißt, er weiß; plur. regular, wir wissen, &c.

AN ALPHABETICAL LIST OF THE IRREGULAR VERBS.

INFINITIVE.	IMPERF. Ind.	PARTICIPLE.
Backen, to bake	buk	gebacken
Befehlen, to command	befahl	befohlen
Befleißen (sich), to apply one's self	befliß	beflissen
Beginnen, to begin	begann	begonnen
Beißen, to bite	biß	gebissen
Bergen, to conceal	barg	geborgen
Bersten, to burst	{ barst / borst }	geborsten
Besinnen sich, to recollect one's self	besann	besonnen
Besitzen, to possess	besaß	besessen
Betrügen, to deceive	betrog	betrogen
Bewegen, to induce	bewog	bewogen
Biegen, to bend	bog	gebogen
Bieten, to bid	bot	geboten
Binden, to bind	band	gebunden
Bitten, to beg	bat	gebeten
Blasen, to blow	blies	geblasen
Bleiben, to remain	blieb	geblieben
Bleichen, to fade	blich	geblichen
Braten, to roast	briet	gebraten
Brechen, to break	brach	gebrochen
Brennen, to burn	brannte	gebrannt
Bringen, to bring	brachte	gebracht
Denken, to think	dachte	gedacht
Dingen, to bargain, hire	dung	gedungen
Dreschen, to thrash	drosch	gedroschen
Dringen, to urge	drang	gedrungen
Empfangen, to receive	empfing	empfangen
Empfehlen, to recommend	empfahl	empfohlen

F

INFINITIVE.	IMPERF. Ind.	PARTICIPLE.
Empfinden, to perceive	empfand	empfunden
Entrinnen, to escape	entrann	entronnen
Erbleichen, to grow pale	erblich	erblichen
Ergreifen, to seize	ergriff	ergriffen
Erküren, to choose	erkor	erkoren
Erlöschen, to become extinct	erlosch	erloschen
Erschallen, to sound	erscholl	erschollen
Erschrecken, to be frightened	erschrak	erschrocken
Erwägen, to consider	erwog	erwogen
Essen, to eat	aß	gegessen
Fahren, to drive, to go in a vehicle	fuhr	gefahren
Fallen, to fall	fiel	gefallen
Fangen, to catch	fing	gefangen
Fechten, to fight	focht	gefochten
Finden, to find	fand	gefunden
Flechten, to twist	flocht	geflochten
Fliegen, to fly	flog	geflogen
Fliehen, to flee	floh	geflohen
Fließen, to flow	floß	geflossen
Fressen, to devour, eat	fraß	gefressen
Frieren, to freeze	fror	gefroren
Gähren, to ferment	gohr	gegohren
Gebären, to bring forth	gebar	geboren
Geben, to give	gab	gegeben
Gebieten, to command	gebot	geboten
Gedeihen, to prosper	gedieh	gediehen
Gehen, to go	ging	gegangen
Gelingen, to succeed (*impers.*)	gelang	gelungen
Gelten, to be worth	galt	gegolten
Genesen, to recover	genas	genesen
Genießen, to enjoy	genoß	genossen

INFINITIVE.	IMPERF. Ind.	PARTICIPLE.
Geſchehen, to happen (*impers.*)	geſchah	geſchehen.
Gewinnen, to gain	gewann	gewonnen
Gießen, to pour	goß	gegoſſen
Gleichen, to be alike	glich	geglichen
Gleiten, to slide	glitt	geglitten
Glimmen, to shine faintly	glomm	geglommen
Graben, to dig	grub	gegraben
Greifen, to seize	griff	gegriffen
Halten, to hold	hielt	gehalten
Hangen, to hang (*int.*)	hing	gehangen
Hauen, to hew	hieb	gehauen
Heben, to lift	hob	gehoben
Heißen, to be called	hieß	geheißen
Helfen, to help	half	geholfen
Keifen, to scold	kiff	gekiffen
Kennen, to know	kannte	gekannt
Klimmen, to climb	klomm	geklommen
Klingen, to sound	klang	geklungen
Kneifen, to pinch	kniff	gekniffen
Kommen, to come	kam	gekommen
Kreiſchen, to cry	kriſch	gekriſchen
Kriechen, to creep	kroch	gekrochen
Laben, to load	lub	gelaben
Laufen, to run	lief	gelaufen
Leiben, to suffer	litt	gelitten
Leißen, to lend	ließ	gelleßen
Leſen, to read	las	geleſen
Liegen, to lie, be situated	lag	gelegen
Lügen, to lie, to utter a falsehood	log	gelogen
Mahlen, to grind	mahlte	gemahlen
Meiben, to avoid	mieb	gemieben

INFINITIVE.	IMPERF. Ind.	PARTICIPLE.
Melken, to milk	molk	gemolken
Messen, to measure	maß	gemessen
Nehmen, to take	nahm	genommen
Nennen, to name	nannte	genannt
Pfeifen, to whistle	pfiff	gepfiffen
Pflegen, to foster	pflog	gepflogen
Preisen, to extol	pries	gepriesen
Quellen, to spring forth	quoll	gequollen
Rathen, to advise	rieth	gerathen
Reiben, to rub	rieb	gerieben
Reißen, to tear	riß	gerissen
Reiten, to ride	ritt	geritten
Rennen, to run	rannte	gerannt
Riechen, to smell	roch	gerochen
Ringen, to wrestle	rang	gerungen
Rinnen, to coagulate	rann	geronnen
Rufen, to call	rief	gerufen
Salzen, to salt	—	gesalzen
Saufen, to drink like brutes	soff	gesoffen
Saugen, to suck	sog	gesogen
Schaffen, to create	schuf	geschaffen
Scheiden, to separate	schied	geschieden
Scheinen, to appear	schien	geschienen
Schelten, to scold	schalt	gescholten
Scheren, to shear	schor	geschoren
Schieben, to shove	schob	geschoben
Schießen, to shoot	schoß	geschossen
Schinden, to flay	schund	geschunden
Schlafen, to sleep	schlief	geschlafen
Schlagen, to beat	schlug	geschlagen
Schleichen, to sneak	schlich	geschlichen
Schleifen, to grind	schliff	geschliffen

INFINITIVE.	IMPERF.	PARTICIPLE.
	Ind.	
Schließen, to shut	schloß	geschlossen
Schlingen, to twine	schlang	geschlungen
Schmeißen, to fling	schmiß	geschmissen
Schmelzen, to melt	schmolz	geschmolzen
Schneiden, to cut	schnitt	geschnitten
Schrauben, to screw	schrob	geschroben
Schreiben, to write	schrieb	geschrieben
Schreyen, to cry	schrie	geschrieen
Schreiten, to stride	schritt	geschritten
Schwären, to fester	schwor	geschworen
Schweigen, to be silent	schwieg	geschwiegen
Schwellen, to swell	schwoll	geschwollen
Schwimmen, to swim	schwamm	geschwommen
Schwinden, to vanish	schwand	geschwunden
Schwingen, to swing	schwang	geschwungen
Schwören, to swear	schwor, schwur	geschworen
Sehen, to see	sah	gesehen
Senden, to send	sandte	gesandt
Sieden, to boil	sott	gesotten
Singen, to sing	sang	gesungen
Sinken, to sink	sank	gesunken
Sinnen, to meditate	sann	gesonnen
Sitzen, to sit	saß	gesessen
Spalten, to split	—	gespalten
Speyen, to spit	spie	gespieen
Spinnen, to spin	spann	gesponnen
Sprechen, to speak	sprach	gesprochen
Sprießen, to sprout	sproß	gesprossen
Springen, to spring	sprang	gesprungen
Stechen, to sting	stach	gestochen
Stehen, to stand	stand	gestanden
Stehlen, to steal	stahl	gestohlen

INFINITIVE.	IMPERF.	PARTICIPLE.
	Ind.	
Steigen, to mount	stieg	gestiegen
Sterben, to die	starb	gestorben
Stieben, to fly like dust	stob	gestoben
Stinken, to stink	stank	gestunken
Stoßen, to push	stieß	gestoßen
Streichen, to stroke	strich	gestrichen
Streiten, to contend	stritt	gestritten
Thun, to do	that	gethan
Tragen, to carry	trug	getragen
Treffen, to hit	traf	getroffen
Treiben, to drive	trieb	getrieben
Treten, to tread	trat	getreten
Triefen, to drop	troff	getroffen
Trinken, to drink	trank	getrunken
Trügen, to deceive	trog	getrogen
Verbieten, to forbid	verbot	verboten
Verbleichen, to fade	verblich	verblichen
Verderben (*neut.*) to be spoiled	verbarb	verborben
Verdrießen (*imp.*), to vex	verdroß	verdrossen
Vergessen, to forget	vergaß	vergessen
Vergleichen, to compare	verglich	verglichen
Verlieren, to lose	verlor	verloren
Wachsen, to grow	wuchs	gewachsen
Waschen, to wash	wusch	gewaschen
Wägen (*act.*) to weigh	wog	gewogen
Weichen, to yield	wich	gewichen
Weisen, to show	wies	gewiesen
Wenden, to turn (*neut. & refl.*)	wandte	gewandt
Werben, to sue	warb	geworben
Werfen, to throw	warf	geworfen
Wiegen, to weigh (*neut.*)	wog	gewogen
Winden, to wind	wand	gewunden

INFINITIVE.	IMPERF. Ind.	PARTICIPLE.
Wiſſen, to know	wußte	gewußt
Zeihen, to accuse	zieh	geziehen
Ziehen, to draw	zog	gezogen
Zwingen, to compel	zwang	gezwungen

In the list of the irregular verbs, the auxiliary verbs of tenses and moods have been omitted; they will be found in their own places.

Several verbs which have both a transitive and intransitive signification, are regular as transitives, irregular as intransitives. They will be found in the next chapter.

Of a great number of the irregular verbs, compounds have been formed. The simple verbs only will be found in the list; though the compounds share the same irregularities. The following compounds, however, are regular: berennen, to storm; rathſchlagen and berathſchlagen, to counsel; willfahren, to comply with. Also, veranlaſſen, to occasion (from Anlaß, occasion), is regular.

Bewegen, to move (physically, e.g. a table); bleichen, to bleach; pflegen, to be accustomed; ſchleifen, to demolish, to drag along; ſchaffen, to procure; weichen, to soften, are regular with these significations; but with the significations which have been given in the list, they are irregular.

INTRANSITIVE OR NEUTER VERBS.

Intransitive or neuter verbs are those which either ascribe to the subject a *state, condition,* which is neither active nor passive, or express an action which does not pass over to an object. Of the first description, are: ich ſchlafe, I sleep; ich ſtehe, I stand; ich ruhe, I rest; ich ſitze, I sit, &c ; Of the second description are: ich gehe, I walk;

ich kämpfe, I fight ; ich reite, I ride ; ich rede, I speak, &c.
When the time, during which such a state lasts, or the
object of an action which does not pass over to the object, is mentioned, it is expressed by the accusative case :
as, ich schlafe die ganze Nacht, I sleep the whole night; ich
sitze eine Stunde, I sit an hour ; ich gehe eine Meile, I walk a
mile ; ich kämpfe einen guten Kampf, I fight a good fight ;
ich reite ein weißes Pferd, I ride a white horse; ich rede eine
verständliche Sprache, I speak an intelligible language.

From their nature they cannot have a passive voice.
Some of those, however, which express an action, occur
in the passive form, as impersonal verbs, like the Latin
venitur, ventum est, itur, festinatur : as, es wird geredet,
gesungen, gespielt, &c.

The following have both a transitive and intransitive
signification. In the transitive signification they are regular ; in the intransitive irregular :—

TRANSITIVE.	IMP. & PART.	INTRANSITIVE.	IMP. & PART.
Backen,	backte,	Backen,	buk,
to bake.	gebackt.	to be baked.	gebacken.
Braten,	bratete,	Braten,	briet,
to roast.	gebratet.	to roast.	gebraten.
Erschrecken,	erschreckte,	Erschrecken, to	erschrak,
to frighten.	erschreckt.	be frightened.	erschrocken.
Löschen,	löschte,	Erlöschen,	erlosch,
to extinguish.	gelöscht.	to become ex- tinct.	erloschen.
Schmelzen,	schmelzte,	Schmelzen,	schmolz,
to melt.	geschmelzt.	to melt.	geschmolzen.
Schweigen,	schweigte,	Schweigen,	schwieg,
to silence.	geschweigt.	to be silent.	geschwiegen.
Schwellen, to	schwellte,	Schwellen,	schwoll,
cause to swell.	geschwellt.	to swell.	geschwollen.

TRANSITIVE.	IMP. & PART.	INTRANSITIVE.	IMP. & PART,
Sieben,	siebete,	Sieben,	sott,
to boil.	gesiebet.	to boil.	gesotten.
Verberben,	verberbte,	Verberben,	verbarb,
to destroy.	verberbt.	to be spoiled.	verborben.
Verwirren,	verwirrte,	Verwirren,	verworr,
to confuse.	verwirrt.	to be confused.	verworren.
Wenben,	wenbete,	Wenben,	wanbte,
to turn.	gewenbet.	to turn.	gewanbt.

Some intransitives are used as reflectives in phrases
like the following: er arbeitet unb läuft fich tobt, he kills
himself by working and running; viele Menschen spielen
fich arm, many people become poor by gambling; er hat
fich krank getrunken, he has become ill by drinking; er
schläft fich bumm, he becomes stupid by sleeping too much;
biefer hat fich müde gestanben, unb jener steif gesessen, the former
has become tired by standing, and the latter stiff by
sitting: biefer Mann stecht fich gut, this man is well off.

Some intransitives are conjugated with haben, others
with seyn, others with haben and seyn.

1. With haben: all those which express an active state,
or a motion of the subject, without reference to a place,
or without changing its state or condition: as, ich habe
gearbeitet, I have worked; ich habe gefehlt, I have erred; ich
habe geritten, I have taken a ride; ich habe gesprungen, I
have jumped; bas Pferb hat ausgeschlagen, the horse has
kicked.

Note.—The following, however, are always conjugated
with seyn: folgen, to follow; gehen, to go; kommen, to
come; weichen, to yield, to give way; begegnen, to happen;
bleiben, to remain; gelingen (impers.), to succeed; geschehen,
to come to pass.

2. With seyn: all those which express an inactive state

of the subject or a motion, with reference to place or dis-
tance, or a change or transition from one state into another : ich war eingeschlafen, I had fallen asleep ; es ist nicht
gut ausgefallen, it has not turned out well ; die Blume ist ver-
blühet, the flower has faded ; der Baum ist ausgeschlagen, the
tree has got buds ; ich bin nach London geritten, I have rode
to London ; unsere Freunde sind gestern abgereiset, our friends
departed yesterday. In the same way the following ; aus-
arten, to degenerate ; erblassen, to grow pale ; erkalten, to
grow cold ; erröthen, to blush ; erschrecken, to be frightened ;
genesen, to recover ; gerathen, to get into, also, to succeed ;
schwellen, to swell ; verarmen, to grow poor ; verhungern,
to famish with hunger ; verschwinden, to disappear ;
wachsen, to grow ; sterben, to die ; entschlafen, to expire ;
umkommen, to perish.

3. Some of those which express motion are conjugated
with haben and seyn ; with haben, when a reference to time
or manner is expressed ; with seyn, when a reference to a
place or space is denoted ; ich habe lange geritten, I have
rode long ; ich habe schlecht geritten, I have rode badly ; der
Knabe hat geschwind gesprungen, the boy has jumped fast ;
ich bin nach Brighton geritten, I have rode to Brighton ; der
Knabe ist vom Baume gesprungen, the boy has leaped from the
tree.

REFLECTIVE VERBS.

Verbs expressing an action, the subject and object of
which are identical, are called reflective. Most of the
transitive verbs are, therefore, capable of being made
reflectives : as, ich wasche mich, I wash myself ; er liebt sich,
he loves himself. There are, however, in German,
several verbs which are only reflectives, having no meaning without the reflective pronoun, like the English ; I

betake myself, I bethink myself. Most of them require the pronoun in the accusative case.

The following require the pronoun in the dative :—

Sich anmaßen, to presume.   Sich schmeicheln, to flatter one's
— einbilden, to imagine.   self.
— getrauen, to be confident.   — widersprechen, to contra-
                                        dict one's self.

Ich schmeichle mir. Du schmeichelst dir. Er schmeichelt sich, &c.

Note 1.—The reflective form is generally employed in German instead of the passive, when the active object is not expressed : as, das Buch hat sich gefunden, the book has been found ; but not : das Buch hat sich von mir gefunden, for das Buch ist von mir gefunden worden, because the active object, von mir, is expressed ; die Frage beantwortet sich leicht, the question is easily answered ; die Frage wurde von mir beantwortet, the question was answered by me ; dies läßt sich nicht begreifen, that is not to be comprehended ; das versteht sich, that is a matter of course.

2.—The reflective verbs are conjugated with haben ; but several are irregular, and several are compound verbs.

CONJUGATION.
Sich schämen, to be ashamed.

Pres. Ind.	Ich schäme mich.	*Subj.* Ich schäme mich.
	Du schämst dich.	Du schämest dich.
	Er schämt sich.	Er schäme sich.
	Wir schämen uns.	Wir schämen uns.
	Ihr schämt euch.	Ihr schämet euch.
	Sie schämen sich.	Sie schämen sich.
Imperf.	Ich schämte mich.	Ich schämete mich.
Perf.	Ich habe mich geschämt.	Ich habe mich geschämt.
Pluperf.	Ich hatte mich geschämt.	Ich hätte mich geschämt.
1st Fut.	Ich werde mich schämen.	Ich werde mich schämen.
2nd Fut.	Ich werde mich geschämt haben.	Ich werde mich geschämt haben.

1st *Conditional.* Ich würde mich schämen.

2nd ——— Ich würde mich geschämt haben.

Imp. Schäme bu dich.

INFINITIVE.

Pres. Sich schämen.

Perf. Sich geschämt haben.

Fut. Sich schämen werden.

Part. Sich schämend.

IMPERSONAL VERBS.

Verbs which occur only in the form of the third pers. sing., the subject of which is expressed by the indefinite pronoun es, are properly called impersonal: as, es regnet, it rains ; es schneyt, it snows; es bonnert, it thunders ; es blitt, it lightens ; es friert, it freezes ; es thaut, it thaws ; es hagelt, it hails ; es reift, there is a hoar frost ; es durstet mich, or mich durstet, I am thirsty ; es hungert mich, or mich hungert, I am hungry; es friert mich, or mich friert, I am chilled ; es schaubert mich, or mich schaubert, I shudder ; es graut mir (mich), or mir (mich) graut, I am afraid. Some verbs assume the form of impers. verbs: es freuet mich, I rejoice ; es däucht mir, es dünkt mich, it seems to me (the former is preferred when we speak of ideas, the latter when of visible objects ; dieser Satz, däucht mir, enthält Wahrheit, it seems to me that this sentence contains truth; mich.dünkt, diese Farbe ist mehr roth als braun, it seems to me that this colour is more red than brown) ; es ahnt mir, I forebode ; es beliebt mir, I please (wenn Ihnen beliebt, if you please) ; es gelüstet mich, I covet ; es gilt, it concerns ; es heißt, it is said ; es scheint, it appears ; es giebt (from geben) (French *il y a*), there is or are. The last phrase expresses an indefinite existence: as, es giebt Menschen, welche nicht sehen können, there are men who cannot see ; es giebt

viele Menschen in London, welche am Morgen nicht wissen, womit
sie sich den Tag über nähren sollen, there are many people in
London who do not know in the morning wherewith they
shall support themselves during the day.

Most of the imp. verbs are conjugated with haben, very
few with seyn, like geschehen: es ist geschehen, it has happened ; es bonnert, es bonnerte, es hat gebonnert, es hatte gebonnert, es wird bonnern, &c.

Note.—Of a few verbs, impers. reflectives have been
formed: es giebt sich, it will come; es fragt sich, it is the
question ; es sieht sich an, it may be looked at ; es gehört sich,
it behoves.

> Das Spiel des Lebens sieht sich heiter an,
>
> Wenn man den sichern Schatz im Herzen trägt.
>
> *Schiller's Wallenstein.*

COMPOUND VERBS.
First Class (separable.)

PREPOSITIONS OR PARTICLES.	COMPOUNDS.	SIMPLE VERBS.
ab (off),	ablegen, to put off.	legen, to lay.
an (on),	anstellen, to institute.	stellen, to place.
auf (up),	aufgehen, to rise.	gehen, to go.
aus (out).	auslassen, to leave out.	lassen, to leave.
bei (by),	beistehen, to assist.	stehen, to stand.
dar, da (there),	darreichen, to offer.	reichen, to reach.
ein (in),	einkaufen, to buy in.	kaufen, to buy.
empor (up),	emporheben, to lift up.	heben, to lift.
fort (on, away),	fortdauern, to continue.	dauern, to last.
heim (home),	heimkehren, to return.	kehren, to turn.
her (along, towards you),	herbringen, to bring along.	bringen, to bring.
hin (along, from you).	hinbringen, to take along.	bringen, to bring.

G

PREPOSITIONS OR PARTICLES.	COMPOUNDS.	SIMPLE VERBS.
mit (with).	mitnehmen, to take with you.	nehmen, to take.
nach (after).	nachfolgen, to follow after.	folgen, to follow.
nieder (down).	niederlegen, to lay down.	legen, to lay.
ob (on).	obliegen, to be incumbent on, (impers.)	liegen, to lie.
um (signifies loss. eliptically used).	umkommen, to perish. i. e. ums Leben kommen,	kommen, to come.
vor (before).	vorgeben, to pretend.	geben, to give.
weg (away).	wegbleiben, to stay away.	bleiben, to stay.
zu (to).	zureden, encourage.	reden, to speak.
zurück (back).	zurückrufen, to recall.	rufen, to call.
zusammen, (together).	zusammensetzen, to put together.	setzen, to put.

All verbs compounded with these prepositions and particles are separable; and the prefixes, when separated, stand, not only after the verb, but also after all the words in the sentence which are governed by, or depend on, it. The separation takes place in the imperative, in the present and imperfect, unless such a pronoun or conjunction as removes the verb to the end of the sentence, begin the same: as, stehe deinem Nächsten in der Noth bey, assist thy neighbour in his distress; die Sonne ging diesen Morgen um sechs Uhr auf, the sun rose this morning at six o'clock. The augment ge of the pret. participle and the preposition zu, by which a supine is formed of the infinitive, stand between the prefix and verb; and though the preposition zu is never joined to an infinitive of a simple verb, it always coalesces with the verb and the prefix into one word: die Sonne ist schön aufgegangen, the sun has risen beautifully; es ist Zeit anzufangen, it is time to begin.

By the following compound prefixes, compound verbs separable are formed : anheim, bevor, babei, baher, bahin, bavon, einher, herab, hinab, heran, hinan, heraus, hinaus, herbei, herein, hinein, herüber, hinüber, herum, herunter, hinunter, hervor, herzu, hinzu, umher, umhin, voran, voraus, vorbei, vorüber, überein : as, anheimstellen, to refer to ; ich stelle anheim, ich habe anheimgestellt. Her, signifies towards you, hin, from you.

<h3>SECOND CLASS (inseparable.)</h3>

These verbs are formed by prefixing be, er, ver, ent, zer, miß, hinter, and wiber to simple verbs.

PREPOSITIONS, OR PARTICLES.	COMPOUNDS.	SIMPLE VERBS.
be,	beweisen, to prove ;	weisen, to shew.
ent,	entehren, to dishonour ;	ehren, to honour.
emp,	empfangen, to receive ;	fangen, to catch.
er,	erhalten, to preserve ;	halten, to hold.
hinter,	hintergehen, to deceive ;	gehen, to go.
miß,	mißfallen, to displease ;	fallen, to fall.
ver,	vergehen, to pass away ;	gehen, to go.
wiber,	wiberrathen, to dissuade ;	rathen, to advise.
zer,	zerstreuen, to disperse ;	streuen, to strew.

These prepositions and particles are unaccented, and never disjoined from the verb. The verbs, composed with them, do not take the augment ge in the pret. participle ; and the zu of the supine stands before the compounds as before the simple verbs ; ich empfange ; ich habe beinen Brief empfangen; ich hatte das Vergnügen, beinen Brief zu empfangen.

<h3>THIRD CLASS (separable and inseparable).</h3>

The prefixes of these verbs are all prepositions, except wieber, again, which is an adverb. When the verb is separable, the prefix has the accent; when inseparable, it is unaccented. The separables are treated like those of the 1st Class, and the inseparables like those of the 2nd.

SEPARABLE.	INSEPARABLE.
Durchbringen, to force through, part. burchgebrungen.	Durchbringen, to penetrate, part. burchbrungen.
Durchreiſen, to travel through, part. burchgereiſet.	Durchreiſen, to traverse, part. burchreiſet.
Ueberſetzen, to leap over, part. übergeſetzt.	Ueberſetzen, to translate, part. überſetzt.
Uebergehen, to go over, part. übergegangen.	Uebergehen, to pass over, part. übergangen.
Umgehen, to make a roundabout way; also, to have intercourse, part. umgegangen.	Umgehen, to avoid, part. umgangen.
Umkleiden, to change dress, part. umgekleidet.	Umkleiden, to clothe, part. umkleibet.
Unterhalten, to keep under, part. untergehalten.	Unterhalten, to entertain, part. unterhalten.
Unterſchieben, to shove under, part. untergeſchoben.	Unterſchieben, to substitute falsely. part. unterſchoben.
Un·ergehen, to perish. part. untergegangen.	Unternehmen, to undertake, part. unternommen.
Wiederholen, to fetch back, part. wiedergeholt.	Wiederholen, to repeat, part. wiederholt.

THE ADVERBS.

1. An Adverb is a part of speech which defines or

modifies a verb, an adjective, or another adverb. The following classes of adverbs may be formed:—1. Of place: hier, here; wo, where; dort, there; &c.—2. Of time: jetzt, now; gestern, yesterday; oft, often; &c.—Of number and order: einmal, once; erstens, first; &c.— 4.—Of quantity: viel, much; genug, enough; &c.—5. Of manner and quality: weise, wisely; langsam, slowly.— 6. Of doubt: vielleicht, perhaps; &c.—7. Of affirmation and negation: ja, yes; wahrlich, truly; gewiß, certainly; nein, no; nicht, not.—8. Of interrogation: wie? how? &c.—9. Of comparison; sehr, very; mehr, more.

2. Almost all adjectives are now employed as adverbs of manner and quality without undergoing any alteration: as, dieser Mann handelt klug, this man acts prudently; er rennet schnell, he runs fast.

3. The adverbial idea of a sentence was formerly, most frequently, expressed by the genitive case; many adverbs, therefore, retain the characteristic letter of that case; and even substantives and adjectives, or numerals in the form of the genitive, are used as adverbs: bereits, already; stets, constantly; besonders, particularly; anders, otherwise; vergebens, in vain; bestens, in the best manner; schönstens, in the finest manner; ehestens, soonest; erstens, in the first place; glücklicherweise, fortunately; folgender- maßen, in the following manner; einigermaßen, in some measure; meistentheils, for the most part; allenfalls, at all events; keinesweges, by no means; unterweges, on the way; vielmals, many times.

4. Some substantives of the feminine gender, or used in the plural number, take, contrary to rule, s at the end, when they are, for the sake of forming adverbs, composed with adjectives or pronouns: meinerseits (die Seite), on my part; diesseits, on this side; jenseits, on that side; allerseits,

on all parts; beiderſeits, on both sides; allerdings (die Dinge), by all means; ſchlechterdings, by any means.

5. Adverbs of manner and quality, and a few of indefinite time and of quantity: as, bald, soon; oft, often; ſelten, seldom; viel, much; wenig, little; admit the degrees of comparison.

Both degrees are formed in the same way as those of adjectives: ſchöner, ſeltener (ſeltner), ſchönſt, ſeltenſt. But there is a difference between the superlative of comparison and the superlative of eminence.

The superlative of *comparison* does not differ from the predicative form of that of the adj. with am: am ſchönſten: as, er ſchreibt am ſchönſten, i. e. ſchöner als andre, he writes most beautifully, i. e. more beautifully than others; er redete mich am freundlichſten an, i. e. freundlicher als andere, he addressed me most friendly, i. e. more friendly than others; ich war am höchſten erfreuet, i. e. höher als andere, I was most highly rejoiced, i. e. more highly than others.

The superlative of *eminence* is either the superlative in its original form, freundlichſt, höchſt; or that form, preceded by the preposition auf, and the definite article das contracted into aufs, with the termination of the acc. neuter in the 2nd form of inflection: as, er redete mich höflichſt an, or er redete mich aufs höflichſte an, he addressed me most politely, i. e. with the greatest politeness; ich grüße Sie freundlichſt, or aufs freundlichſte, I send you my most friendly compliments. This superlative, however, is also produced by putting höchſt or äußerſt before the adverb: ich wurde äußerſt freundlich von ihm empfangen, I was received by him in an extremely friendly manner; er kommt äußerſt ſelten zu mir, he comes very seldom to me; er beträgt ſich höchſt artig gegen mich, he behaves very politely towards me.

Note.—The termination ens is added to the original

form of the superlative of several words, to express the superlative of eminence: as, höchſtens, at the highest: meiſtens, at most; wenigſtens, at least; ſpäteſtens, at the latest.

The following are irregular:—

Bald, soon ;	*comp.* eher,	*sup.* am eheſten.
Gern, willingly ; —	lieber,	— am liebſten.
Viel, much ; —	mehr,	— am meiſten.
Wenig, little ; —	minder or —	am mindeſten.
	weniger,	or am wenigſten.
Wohl, well ; —	beſſer,	— am beſten.

PREPOSITIONS WHICH GOVERN THE GENITIVE CASE.

Anſtatt, or ſtatt, instead of: it is sometimes separated by the insertion of the case which it governs; an des Vaters Statt, instead of the father.

Halben or halber, on account of, for the sake of. Halben is preferred when the substantive to which it belongs, is preceded by an article or pronoun; otherwise halber: they always stand after the case which they govern. It occurs abbreviated in:

Außerhalb, without, on the outside of.
Innerhalb, within, in the inner part of.
Oberhalb, above, on the upper side of.
Unterhalb, below, on the lower side of.

Diesſeits, on this side of; diesſeits des Fluſſes, on this side of the river.

Jenſeits, on the farther side of: jenſeits des Fluſſes.

Kraft, by the power of, by, or in virtue of.

Laut, according to, conformably to.

Trotz, in spite of: trotz meines Verbotes, in spite of my prohibition.

Vermittelſt, by means of.

Um=willen, for the sake of; the case which it governs always stands between the two words: um des Friedens willen, for the sake of peace.

Ungeachtet, notwithstanding, may precede or follow its case.

Unweit, near, not far from.

Vermöge, by dint of, by the power of, by means of: vermöge der Uebung, by dint of practice.

Während, during: während des Krieges, during the war.

Wegen, because of, on account of, concerning.

Längs, along; längs der Küste, along the coast.

Zufolge, in consequence of, governs the genitive when it precedes its case, and the dative when it follows it; zufolge des Befehles, in consequence of the order; dem Befehle zufolge.

Außer governs the genitive case in one instance; außer Landes, out of the country.

PREPOSITIONS WHICH GOVERN THE DATIVE CASE.

Aus :—1. out of; er kommt aus dem Hause, he comes out of the house :—2. from, aus Eitelkeit freigebig, liberal from vanity.

Außer, out of, on the outside of; der Kranke ist jetzt außer Gefahr, the patient is at present out of danger.

Bei, by, near, with, on, at; ich stand bei dem Könige, I stood near the king; er wohnt bei seinem Bruder, he lives with his brother; bei meiner Ankunft, on my arrival; beim Tode seines Vaters, at the death of his father.

Binnen, within; binnen 24 Stunden, within 24 hours.

Entgegen :—1. opposite to: der Strom ist uns entgegen, the tide is against us ;—2. towards, so as to meet, united with verbs implying motion : er kam mir entgegen, he came to meet me.   It always stands after the case.

Gegenüber, over against, opposite to : der Kirche gegenüber, opposite the church ; it stands after the case.

Längs, along : längs dem Fluſſe ; sometimes used with the genitive.

Mit, with ; ich habe noch niemals mit dieſem Manne geſprochen, I have never yet spoken to this man.

Nach, after, to, according to ; nach Neujahr, after New-year's-day : wir gehen nach der Stadt, we go to town ; meiner Meinung nach, in my opinion. In the latter signification, it may be put after the substantive.

Nebſt, together with ; meine beiden Nachbarn nebſt meinen Söhnen waren geſtern Abend bei mir, both my neighbours together with my sons, were with me last night.

Ob, over, at, on account of, is used only in poetry : alle Redlichen beklagen ſich ob dieſes Landvogts Geize (*Schiller's Tell*), every honest man complains of the avarice of this governor.

Sammt, together with ; Aaron ſammt ſeinen Söhnen ſollen ihre Hände auf ſein Haupt legen (Exod. xxix. 15).

Seit, since ; ſeit dem Tode ſeines Kindes fühlt der Vater ſich unglücklich, since the death of his child, the father feels unhappy.

Von, from, of, by ; das Buch iſt von einem Biſchof geſchrieben, the book is written by a bishop.

Zu, to, at, for, ich will zu meinem Nachbar gehen ; mein Schneider wird morgen zu mir kommen.

Zufolge, in consequence of, according to, governs the dative when it stands after the substantive.

Zuwider, against, in opposition to, always stands after the case : den Geſetzen zuwider.

Note.—Several of these prepositions occur in the following lines :—

Nach dir schmacht' ich, zu dir eil' ich, du geliebte Quelle du!
Aus dir schöpf' ich, bey dir ruh' ich, seh' dem Spiel der Wellen zu.
Mit dir scherz' ich, von dir lern' ich, heiter durch das Leben wallen,
Angelacht von Frühlingsblumen, und begrüßt von Nachtigallen.

PREPOSITIONS WHICH GOVERN THE ACCUSATIVE CASE.

Bis, till : ich blieb gestern Abend bis zehn Uhr bei meinem
Freunde, I stayed last night till ten o'clock with my friend;
it occurs with the prepositions an, auf, über, nach, in, zu ;
but when it is followed by other prepositions, the case of
the substantive following is governed by them: bis an die
Stadt, as far as the town.

Durch, through ; as, der König ist durch die Stadt gekom=
men ; viele Menschen bereichern sich durch den Handel, many
men enrich themselves by trade ; die ganze Nacht durch, all
the night through. In this signification hindurch is also
used : das ganze Jahr hindurch.

Für, for : meine Freunde haben alle für mich gestimmt, all my
friends have voted for me.

Gegen, to, towards, against ; mein Nachbar ist freundlich
gegen mich gesinnt, my neighbour is kindly disposed towards
me ; gegen Schwache sollte man immer nachsichtig seyn, one
ought always to be indulgent to the weak.

Ohne, without ; ohne mich, without me ; ohne meinen
Beistand, without my assistance.

Um, around, about, for ; wir gingen um den Kirchhof, we
went round the churchyard ; wir sitzen um den Tisch, we sit
round the table.

Wider, against, in opposition to : wer nicht wider uns
ist, der ist für uns (Luke ix. 50).

Note.—In the following lines, several of these prepositions occur :—

Philemon an seinen Freund.

Durch Dich ist die Welt mir schön, ohne Dich würd' ich sie hassen;
Für Dich leb' ich ganz allein, um Dich will ich gern erblassen;
Gegen Dich soll kein Verleumder ungestraft sich je vergehn;
Wider Dich kein Feind sich waffnen; ich will Dir zur Seite stehn.

PREPOSITIONS WHICH GOVERN THE DATIVE AND ACCUSATIVE CASES.

Preliminary Remark.

The prepositions contained in this chapter, govern the
dative case, when a state of permanent locality is implied;
but the accusative case when a motion from one place or
object to another is denoted. This motion can be physical or mental; for our thoughts proceed from us, and
pass over to an object; ich denke an ihn, I think of him;
wir glauben an den Sohn Gottes, we believe in the Son of
God. Permanent locality does not exclude motion within
a place; it only excludes motion from one place or object
to another: e. g. ich gehe im Zimmer, means, I walk in the
room; but, ich gehe ins Zimmer, I walk into the room; ich
springe auf dem Stuhle, I am on the chair jumping; ich
springe auf den Stuhl, I jump on the chair.

An, with the dative, *of, in, on, near, at:* das Haus
meines Bruders steht an dem Ufer eines Flusses.

An, with the accusative expresses: *motion* from one
place or subject to another; either bodily or mental: ich
stelle den Tisch an die Wand, I put the table against the wall.

Auf, on, upon, with the dative, denotes permanent locality in reference to a higher place, or the upper side of
things: das Buch liegt auf dem Tische (not an dem Tische),
the book lies upon the table.

Auf, with the accusative has the same significations as

auf with the dative, but it is only employed when a motion from one place to another is denoted; id) lege bas Buch auf ben Tijd), I put the book on the table.

Hinter, behind, with the dative, denotes permanent locality; er ftebt hinter mir, he stands behind me.

Hinter, with the accusative case, denotes motion: plöglich trat er hinter mich, um mich zu erschrecken, suddenly he stept behind me, to terrify me.

In, in, with the dative, denotes permanent locality, within, or in the inside of; id) wohne in ber Stadt, I live in town; biefer Mann ift niemals in meinem Haufe gewefen, this man has never been in my house.

In, with the accusative, denotes motion into: wir fürchten uns in ein folches Haus zu gehen, in welchem eine anftedenbe Krankheit ift, we are afraid of going into such a house, in which there is an infectious disease.

Neben, with the dative, denotes permanent locality, at the side of: er ftanb neben mir, als id) redete, he stood at my side when I spoke.

Neben, with the accusative, denotes motion: er ftellte fich neben mich, um mich zu vertheidigen, he placed himself at my side to defend me.

Ueber, with the dative, denotes permanent locality, over, above; ber Bogel fchwebt über bem Haufe, the bird soars over the house.

Ueber, with the accusative, denotes motion over: id) gehe täglich zweimal über bie Brücke, I go every day twice over the bridge.

Unter, with the dative, permanent locality, under, beneath; id) ftanb eine Stunde unter einem Baume, um nicht naß zu werden, I stood an hour under a tree, not to get wet.

Unter, with the accusative, denotes motion, under, beneath: id) trat unter einen Baum, als es anfing zu regnen,

I stepped under a tree when it began to rain.

Bor, with the dative, denotes before; ich ſtand vor dem Hauſe, als mein Freund ankam, I was standing before the house, when my friend arrived.

Bor, with the accusative, denotes motion before: ich trat vor den Mann, I stepped before the man.

Zwiſchen, with the dative, denotes permanent locality between: ich ſaß zwiſchen zwei Freunden, I sat between two friends.

Zwiſchen, with the accusative, denotes motion between: ſage ihm, daß er ſich zwiſchen mich und dich ſetze, tell him to seat himself between me and thee.

Note.—Several of these prepositions occur in the fol-. lowing lines:—

An den Mond.

Auf dich blicket, auf dir weilet oft mein Aug' in ſüßer Luſt;
An dir haft' ich, an dich ſend ich manch Gefühl aus froher Bruſt.
In dich ſetzet, in dir findet meine Phantaſie viel Scenen,
Unter die ſie gern ſich träumet, unter denen dort die ſchönen
Seelen, über dieſe Erd' erhöhet, über Gräbern wandeln.
Vor mich tritt dann, vor mir ſteht dann der Entſchluß, recht gut
    zu handeln.
Zwiſchen dieſen Sträuchen ſitz' ich, zwiſchen ſie ſtiehlt ſich dein
    Strahl.
Neben mich ſinkt, neben mir ruht ſie, die Freundinn meiner
    Wahl;
Hinter mich ſtill hingeſchlichen, ſtand ſie lachend hinter mir,
Und wir reden von den Sternen, unſern Lieben und von dir.

Note.— Some prepositions coalesce with the definite article (a) an, in, von, zu, in the dative sing. of the masculine and neuter genders, dem, in the following manner: am, im, vom, zum. Some authors contract also über, unter, vor, with that article, into überm, unterm, vorm;

H

(b) ʒu, in the dative sing. of the feminine ber into ʒur.
In ancient writings, ʒun occurs for ʒu ben; (c) an, auf,
burch, für, über, unter, vor, in the accusative of the neuter,
into ans, aufs, burchs, fürs, übers, unters, vors. The con-
traction cannot take place with the demonstrative pronoun bem, bas, because it has a peculiar accent.

THE CONJUNCTIONS.

Conjunctions are parts of speech which connect words
and sentences, and express the relations of one sentence
to another.   Those marked (*) in the subjoined list,
remove the copula to the end of the sentence; those
marked (§) have, as adverbs, their proper place after the
copula, and therefore remove the subject after the
copula when they are put before the subject.——(See the
arrangement of words). The following five always stand
at the beginning of a sentence, without affecting the
order of the words : allein, benn (in the signification of
for), fonbern, unb, ober.

Aber and allein, but.——Aber does not always place the
sentences in opposition ; it expresses in the most indefinite way, what is not *necessarily* inferred from the antecedent : bie Könige im Lanbe lehnen fich gegen ben Herrn
auf; aber ber im Himmel wohnet lachet ihrer, the kings of
the earth set themselves against the Lord, but he that
sitteth in heaven laughs at them.

Allein expresses the contrary of what might be inferred
from the antecedent : ber Knabe ift fehr fleißig, allein er lernt
wenig.

    * Als : — 1. as : — 2. than : — 3. but, after nichts,
nothing : — 4. when, referring to a definite event of past
time.

    Auch, also : So—auch, however : fo fpät es auch ift, fo

muß ich doch ausgehen, however late it is, yet I must go out.

* Auf daß, in order that, synonymous with damit, expresses design or purpose.

Außer denotes except: ich sah niemand außer ihn, I saw nobody except him.

§ Außerdem, besides.

* Bevor, before, refers to time only.

* Bis, until : höre nicht auf zu lernen, bis du es weißt.

* Da, since, as, implies a logical cause from which an inference is drawn: da der Wind im Osten ist, so wird es wohl trocken bleiben, as the wind is in the east, it will perhaps remain dry.

§ Daher, therefore, expresses a physical cause.

* Dafern, if, in case that. (Not much in use.)

* Damit, in order that.

§ Dann (or alsdann, denn), then, expresses time: erst arbeite, dann spiele, first work, then play.

§ Darum, deßwegen, deßhalb (derohalben is antiquated), on that account; each of these expresses a motive or a moral cause.

* Daß, that; this conjunction is much more frequently used in German than in English. Many subordinate sentences require this conjunction and the finite verb, which are in English expressed either by an accusative case and the infinitive mood, or by a participle used substantively: as, I know him to be the man, ich weiß, daß er der Mann ist; there is no doubt of his having acted a bad part, es ist kein Zweifel daran, daß er eine schlechte Rolle gespielt hat; I insist upon his paying me the money, ich bestehe darauf, daß er mir das Geld bezahlt.

Denn:—1. for, because, expresses a reason;—2. it occurs in the phrase: es sey denn, daß, unless;—3. than, after a comparative degree; but not so common as als, unless another als occurs in the same sentence.

§ Dennoch, deffenungeachtet, and nichtsdeftoweniger, not-withstanding, nevertheless, still ; state a consequence or effect which might not be inferred from the antecedent.

§ Deßgleichen and ingleichen, likewise. (Deffelbigengleichen is antiquated.)

§ Defto, see je.

* Dieweil, because, is obsolete.

Doch, yet, still, though, states :—1. a cause or motive which might not be inferred from the antecedent, or ex-presses a condition : biefer Mann ift fehr reich, und hat doch wenig gearbeitet, this man is very rich, and yet has worked little ;—2. it is used as an adverb to strengthen an affir-mation, negation, request, complaint, wish, &c., and is to be translated by : to be sure, certainly, sometimes by pray; habe ich doch nie fo etwas gefehn! to be sure, I have never seen such a thing.

* Ehe, before : ich will zu Ihnen kommen, ehe ich nach Haufe gehe.

§ Einerfeits, andrerfeits, on the one side, on the other side.

§ Endlich, at length.

Entweder, either, always followed by oder, or : entweder du oder ich.

* Falls, in case that : falls es gefchehen follte.

§ Ferner, farther, moreover, synonymous with weiter.

§ Folglich, consequently, synonymous with alfo.

Gleichfam, as it were, (Lat. quasi).

§ Gleichwohl and indeffen, yet, however, nevertheless. They state, like dennoch, a consequence or effect which might not be inferred from the antecedent, but not so positively.

§ Hernach and nachher, afterwards. Hernach merely de-notes future time : ich kann bir bas Buch jetzt nicht geben, du follst es hernach haben. Nachher expresses future time in re-ference to another event : anfangs wollte er mir den Umftand nicht mittheilen, aber nachher that er es doch.

Hingegen and dagegen, on the other hand.

* Je, stands, like the definite article in English, before a comparative degree when two are brought together for the purpose of expressing an equal degree of quality or manner, and is followed by besto; je fleißiger ein Knabe ist, besto gelehrter wird er, the more industrious a boy is, the more learned he becomes ; je öfter ich es thue, besto leichter wird es mir, the more frequently I do it, the easier it is to me. The sentence with besto may precede that with je in the following manner: ein Mensch ist besto größer in Gottes Augen, je demüthiger und bescheidener er ist, a man is the greater in God's eyes, the humbler and the more modest he is. Instead of besto, je is used when not an equal, but only a mutual, degree is expressed : komm je eher, je lieber, come, the sooner the better. Desto also stands before a comparative degree, to denote proportion, without je and another comparative preceding ; ich erwartete nicht meinen Freund zu finden, besto größer aber war meine Freude, als ich ihn sah, I did not expect to find my friend, but my joy was the greater when I saw him. In this signification, um so, or um so viel, is also used instead of besto; du hast es nicht gethan, und das ist mir um so lieber, you have not done it, and that is so much the more agreeable to me.

§ Jedoch, yet, states, in an indefinite manner, what might not be inferred from the antecedent: er wird es thun können, jedoch nicht ohne Mühe, he will be able to do it, yet not without trouble.

* Je nachdem, according as, expresses a degree, which changes according to another circumstance: du erhältst Lob, je nachdem du fleißig bist.

* Indem denotes :—1. while ; and is used to state an event which is simultaneous with another ; indem wir auf= und abgingen, trat ein fremder Mann zu uns, while we walked

up and down, a strange man walked up to us :—2. since ; stating a cause in an indefinite manner ; der Frankfurter Kaufmann war diesen Morgen in meinem Hause, aber er ging gleich wieder weg, indem er mich nicht zu Hause fand.

§ Indessen or indeß, denotes :—1. in the meantime ; indessen hoben sie ihre Augen auf, und sahen einen Haufen Ismaeliter kommen (Gen. xxxvii. 25) :—2. however ; er hat nicht viel gethan, ich erwartete indessen nicht mehr von ihm, he has not done much ; however I did not expect more from him.

§ Ingleichen, see deßgleichen.

§ In so fern, in so weit, or so weit, so far ; they are followed by als, as ; ich billige in so fern sein Betragen, als es den Vorschriften des Christenthums nicht zuwider ist, I approve of his behaviour, so far as it is not contrary to the precepts of Christianity.

In wie fern, in wie weit, how far ; in wie fern ist dieses zu billigen ?

§ Kaum, followed by so or als, may be rendered by scarce, followed by when, or by no sooner, followed by than : kaum hat der Mensch einen Wunsch in Erfüllung gehen sehen, so hegt er schon einen neuen, man has no sooner obtained one wish, than he already entertains another ; kaum hatte er mich gesehen, so rief er aus, or als er ausrief, he had no sooner seen me than he exclaimed.

§ Mithin, consequently.

* Nachdem, after, refers to a preceding event, and states that two events have taken place consecutively ; nachdem ich meine Arbeit vollendet hatte, machte ich einen Spaziergang, after I had finished my work, I took a walk.

Nämlich, namely (Lat. *videlicet, viz.*)   In German it is frequently used as an explanative conjunction, where none is employed in English.

§ Nicht allein, nicht nur, nicht bloß, not only ; followed

by ſonbern auch, but also. Nicht allein is used when a mere difference is expressed: er hat nicht allein ſeinen Bruber, ſonbern auch ſeine Schweſter eingelaben. Nicht nur is used when the subsequent member expresses more than the antecedent: er hat ihm nicht nur gebroht, ſonbern ihn auch ge= ſchlagen. Nicht bloß is employed when the subsequent member confirms or strengthens the antecedent: er hat mir nicht bloß Selb verſprochen, ſonbern auch gegeben.

§ Noch, as a conjunction, has a negative power, like the English *nor*, after weber and nicht: weber heute noch morgen, neither to-day nor to-morrow.

* Nun, now, is sometimes used as a conjunction denoting a logical cause, like ba, or an indefinite cause, like inbem.

§ Nur, as a conjunction, is sometimes used in the signification of aber: ich wünſchte es wohl zu haben, nur kann ich es nicht erhalten, indeed I wished to have it, but I cannot get it.

* Db, if, whether, is only used in indirect questions, or before sentences which express doubt or possibility: ich weiß nicht, ob er meine Bitte gewähren wirb, I do not know whether he will grant my request.

* Dbgleich, obſchon, obwohl (in poetry also ob auch), though, although. Dbgleich expresses a certain state or condition in a definite manner; obſchon, in an indefinite manner; obwohl, a state or condition which is only considered as existing. They are frequently separated, especially when a monosyllable follows, such as: ich, bu, er, wir, ihr, ſie.

Dhne, without (see the preposition), is, like außer, used as a conjunction in the signification of, if not, but, save: wo iſt ein Gott, ohne ber Herr? ober ein Hort, ohne unſer Gott? (Ps. xviii. 32); niemanb kann Jeſum einen Herrn nennen, ohne burch ben heiligen Geiſt, no one can say that Jesus is the Lord, but by the Holy Ghost. (1 Cor. xii. 3.)

* Seitdem, since, from the time that, denotes an event, as the beginning of a period into which another event falls : seitdem wir uns sahen, bin ich unwohl gewesen, since we saw each other, I have been unwell.

So, signifies :—1. so, as, denoting a comparison, proportion : wie die Jugend, so das Alter, as youth, so old age; der Knabe ist so gut als das Mädchen, the boy is as good as the girl. Instead of the corresponding word als, so is also used in the following manner : so gelehrt er ist, so anmaßend ist er auch, i. e. er ist so anmaßend als gelehrt :— 2. thus, in this manner, denoting a consequence; thue nichts böses, so wird dir auch nichts böses begegnen. In the last mentioned signification so is employed to connect the principal sentence with the secondary, when the latter begins with a conjunction, such as : wenn, als, da, weil, nachdem, wie, obgleich, obschon, obwohl : wenn mein Bruder kommt, so sage ihm, daß ich bald nach Hause kommen werde, when my brother comes, (the consequence of which shall be) tell him that I shall soon come home;—3. if: so ihr bleiben werdet in meiner Lehre (John viii. 31) :—4. it is, in Luther's translation of the bible, frequently used for the relative pronoun welcher, e, es : auf daß die, so rechtschaffen sind, offenbar werden (1 Cor. xi. 19).

Sondern, but, is used :—1. before the subsequent member of a sentence which negatives either the whole contents, or an idea of the antecedent, and expresses what is different from it ; the antecedent, however, must contain a negative : ich habe ihn nicht gelobt, sondern getadelt; er hat nicht seine Kenntnisse, sondern seinen Fleiß bewundert.

§ Sonst, else, otherwise : wir müssen Bücher haben, sonst können wir nichts lernen, we must have books, otherwise we can learn nothing. Sonst nichts, nothing else.

Sowohl—als, or als auch, as well as : die Armen sind sowohl Gottes Kinder, als die Reichen; die Reichen haben ihre Leiden und Plagen sowohl als die Armen.

§ Theils—theils, partly—partly.

§ Uebrigens, as for the rest, however.

§ Ueberdies, besides.

Und, and.

* Ungeachtet, is used as a conjunction with the significa-tion of obgleich, although : er that es, ungeachtet ich es ihm verboten hatte.

‡ Vielmehr, much more, rather.

* Während, while, during the time that, denotes the duration of an event which is simultaneous with another: viele Menschen lesen die Zeitung, während sie essen, many people read the newspaper while they dine. Weil instead of während, is antiquated.

Warum, weßwegen, weßhalb, why, wherefore.

Wann, when, an interrogative : wann haben sie ihn gesehen ? ich weiß nicht, wann er kommen wird.

Weder, followed by noch, neither, nor : weder der Vater noch der Sohn.

* Weil, because, expresses a moral or real cause in a definite manner : ich will keinen Umgang mit diesem Manne haben, weil er stolz ist, I will have no intercourse with this man, because he is proud ; wir können nicht fliegen, weil wir keine Flügel haben.

* Wenn signifies :—1. when ; and denotes time in the most indefinite manner ; for this reason it is used (a) with the present or future tenses : wenn die Sonne scheint, ist es warm, when the sun shines, it is warm ; wenn ich ihn sehen werde, will ich es ihm sagen; wenn ich meine Arbeit werde vollendet haben, will ich zu dir kommen ; (b) with the imper-fect, denoting an indefinite time : wenn er nach London kam, besuchte er mich, when (i. e. whenever) he came to London, he paid me a visit :—2. if, conditional : wenn du mir das Buch geben willst, so will ich dir dafür danken, if you will give me the book, I will thank you for it ; wenn du fromm bist,

fo biſt bu angenehm (Gen. iv. 7). In this signification, it is frequently omitted, and the sentence assumes the form of an interrogative one: brückt euch ein Kummer, werft ihn friſch vom Herzen (*Schiller's Tell*).

* Wenngleich, wennſchon, wenn auch, although, are synonymous with obgleich, obſchon, obwohl, and are separated in the same way.

* Wie, as, denotes:—1, similarity, whilst als expresses proportion, degree: ſeyd klug, wie die Schlangen, und ohne Falſch, wie die Tauben (Matth. x. 16);—2, when, as, denoting a definite time, like als, especially used with the present tense instead of the imperf. to enliven the narrative: wie er mich ſieht, kennt er mich, when he saw me, he recognised me;—3, how: wie haſt du das gemacht? ich weiß nicht, wie ich es machen ſoll.

* Wie auch, however, generally separated by an adjective or adverb.

* Wiewohl, although.

* Wo, is an adverb of place, where: wo iſt er? ich weiß nicht, wo er iſt. As a conjunction, it signifies *if*, and is sometimes used for wenn: wo du mir das thuſt, ſo ſollſt du nicht wieder in mein Haus kommen, if you do that, you shall not come again into my house. It is rather antiquated, except in the expressions, wo nicht, if not, wo möglich, if possible.

* Wofern, in case that, if: wofern er ſich weigern ſollte, ſo müſſen wir ihn zwingen.

§ Wohl denotes indeed, perhaps (Lat. *quidem*): die Geſchichte iſt wohl wahr, aber ſage nichts davon, the story, indeed, is true, but say nothing of it.

§ Zudem, besides.

§ Zwar, indeed, it is so, allowing it, generally followed by aber, allein, doch, bennoch, or a similar conjunction, in the subsequent member: ich habe es ihm zwar geſagt, aber er hat es nicht verſtanden.

* Obzwar is sometimes met with for obgleich, obschon, although.

THE INTERJECTIONS.

Interjections are sounds produced by the immediate impulse of the sensations of joy, mirth, and gaiety; of sorrow and displeasure; of pain and disgust; of surprise and admiration. The following usually occur in German: —1, to indicate joy, mirth, gaiety: ah! ha! hey! heyssa! juchhey! Gottlob!—2, sorrow and displeasure: ach! ah! oh!—3, pain and disgust: ach! o weh! oh! leider! fi! pfui!—4, surprise and admiration: hem! ah! ha! haha! postausend! o! oh! ey! For calling out a person, the following are used: he! holla! pst!—Pst! Nachbar, ein Wort, Pst! neighbour! one word. (*Göthe's Egmont.*)

Interjections do not govern a case; they may stand before any case according to the construction of the sentence. It is, however, a peculiarity of the German language to put an absolute genitive after o and ach: o, des unglücklichen Mannes!

The words wohl, well; Heil, hail; wehe, woe; are always followed by the dative, which is governed by the verb seyn understood: wohl (ist) dem, der nicht wandelt im Rath der Gottlosen (Ps. i.): Heil (sey) dir, junger Mann! Dein treues Auge, dein treues Herz hat richtig gewählt (*Göthe's Hermann and Dorothea*); wehe dem Menschen, durch welchen des Menschen Sohn verrathen wird.—(Mark xiv. 21.)

ON THE ARRANGEMENT OF WORDS.

The essential parts of a sentence are called *subject* and *predicate*. The *subject* is that, of which something is said (predicated) and *predicate* is that, which is said of the subject. The predicate must not be confounded with the object. A sentence may be formed without an object, but not without a predicate. That word which connects subject and predicate we call *copula*. This copula is always an auxiliary verb of tense or mood. The necessary explanations will be found in the following rules.

1. The order of the words in a simple sentence is:—

Subject.	Copula.	Predicate.
Die Blume	ist	ſchön.

2. A sentence has no copula, when the predicate is expressed by a verb, which is no auxiliary verb, in the present or imperfect tense of the active voice. In this case the verb takes the place of the copula, and the place of the predicate remains vacant:—

Subj.	Cop.	Pred.
Die Blume	blüht	——
Die Knaben	leſen	——

3. The place of the predicate is occupied either by a substantive or an adjective, or a participle, or an infinitive mood, or a particle of a compound verb separable:—

Subj.	Cop.	Pred.
Der Hund	ist	ein Thier.
Die Blume	ist	gelb.
Der Knabe	hat	geſchrieben.
Der Knabe	kann	ſchreiben.
Der Mann	wird	gelobt.
Wir	werden	loben.
Die Ferien	fangen	an.
Ich	gehe	aus.

4. When the verbs which take the place of the copula are used in a compound form, i. e. in the perfect, &c. the inflected parts only take the place of the copula, and the uninflected parts, the participles or infinitives, stand after the predicate:—

Subj.	Cop.	Pred.
Der Mann	ift	thöricht gewesen.
Das Kind	wird	gelesen haben.
Wir	haben	schreiben müssen.
Der Knabe	hat	arbeiten können.
Der Bater	ift	ausgegangen.
Die Ferien	haben	angefangen.

5. The object of the sentence stands between the copula and the predicate.

Subj.	Cop.	Obj.	Pred.
Der Knabe	hat	einen Brief	geschrieben.
Ich	schreibe	einen Brief	————
Er	fängt	seine Arbeit	an.
Sie	haben	Wein	getrunken.
Er	ift	eines Berbrechens	beschuldigt worden.

6. The case of the person stands before that of the thing.

Subj.	Cop.		Pred.
Ich	habe	bem Knaben ein Buch	gegeben.
Wir	müssen	ben Mann seinem Schicksale	überlassen.

7. When two cases are both of person, the accusative precedes the dative:—

Subj.	Cop.		Pred.
Er	hat	seinen Sohn seinem Bedienten anvertraut.	
Ich	habe	beine Tochter meinem Freunde empfohlen.	

But the oblique cases of the personal pronouns always stand before other cases.

Ich	habe	bir	seinen Sohn	empfohlen.
Er	hat	es	meinem Nachbar	erzählt.

8. When there are two personal pronouns in a sentence, the accusative precedes the dative and the genitive:—

Sie	haben	es	mir	gegeben.
Ich	schicke	sie	ihnen	————

I

Er wird sie dir vorstellen

Wir nehmen uns seiner an.

Er hat sich mir empfohlen.

9. Adverbs of manner, or such substantives with pre-positions as may be regarded as adverbs, stand imme-diately before the predicate, or, should the predicate be implied in the verb, before the vacant place.

Subj.	Cop.	Obj.	Adv.	Pred.
Der Mann	hat	seinen Gegenstand	vortrefflich	behandelt.
Der Mann	behandelt	seinen Gegenstand	vortrefflich	——
Ich	habe	das Buch	aufmerksam	gelesen.
Er	hat	das Geld	mit Freuden	ausgegeben.

10. Adverbs of time, and such substantives as may be regarded as adverbs, precede the object unless it is a pronoun, which stands even before adverbs of time; and when the time, denoted by an adverb, is more particu-larly stated by a substantive, the adverb precedes the substantive.

Ich habe gestern einen Brief geschrieben.

Du kannst morgen um zehn Uhr das Geld erhalten.

Viele Leute haben immer des Sonntags Gesellschaft.

Er ist vor drei Tagen in London angekommen.

11. Adverbs of place, and substantives with preposi-tions which may be regarded as adverbs of place, stand between the object and the predicate.

Ich habe die Katze auf dem Hause gesehen.

Wir können das Buch in ganz London nicht erhalten.

Er wird seinen Sohn nach Paris schicken.

Der Mann ließ mich lange an der Thüre warten.

12. The adverbs, nicht, zwar, etwa, wohl, vielleicht, gern, stand immediately before the predicate, when they modify the verb. But when they modify an idea, expressed by another word, they stand before that word. Er hat es mir nicht gesagt. Er hat es nicht mir gesagt. Ich will Ihnen das Buch gern geben. Ich will Ihnen gern das Buch geben.

13. Substantives or pronouns, with such prepositions as the verb of the sentence requires, generally stand immediately before the predicate. When the preposition does not depend upon the verb, but expresses a cause, purpose, &c. the substantive with the preposition generally precedes the object: Ich habe niemals über den Gegenstand mit ihm gesprochen. Wir hätten dieses nicht von dem Manne erwartet. Ich konnte ihm vor Freude keine Antwort geben. Er hat mir zu meiner Freude meine Bitte nicht abgeschlagen.

14. When a particular stress is to be laid on any one of those words which stand after the copula, it is placed before the subject. In this case, subject and copula exchange places. Sie werden morgen einen Brief von Ihrem Vater erhalten. You will receive to-morrow a letter from your father. Morgen werden Sie einen Brief von Ihrem Vater erhalten. Einen Brief werden Sie morgen von Ihrem Vater erhalten. Von Ihrem Vater werden Sie morgen einen Brief erhalten. Erhalten werden Sie morgen einen Brief von Ihrem Vater. In order to lay a particular stress on a word, which has its place between copula and predicate, it may be put before such words as have likewise their place between subject and predicate. Sie werden einen Brief morgen von Ihrem Vater erhalten. Sie werden von Ihrem Vater morgen einen Brief erhalten.

15. The subject stands after the copula: (a) in direct questions, unless the interrogative is the subject: Welches Buch hat der Schüler gelesen? Welcher Schüler ist träge gewesen? (b) In imperative sentences: sagen Sie es ihm selbst. (c) When a wish is expressed by mögen: möge er lange leben. (d) When the conjunction wenn, if, is omitted: wäre das Wetter schön, so ginge ich aus. (e) In expressions of quotation: wir alle, sprach er, sind verloren.

16. The position of all the parts of a simple sentence having been explained, the most essential rules concern-

ing principal and secondary, or subordinate sentences, will be given. When secondary sentences are put before principal sentences, they affect the position of subject and copula in the principal sentence in the same way as a single part, when put before the subject; they make subject and copula to exchange places: wenn ich ihn sehe, werde ich es ihm sagen; if I see him, I shall tell him so; seitdem wir uns gesehen haben, habe ich nichts neues gehört, since we have seen each other, I have heard no news.

17. Observe the difference between real conjunctions and adverbial conjunctions. Adverbial conjunctions, such as, daher, therefore, dessenungeachtet, notwithstanding, have their place, like adverbs, between the copula and predicate, and therefore make subject and copula to exchange places, when they are put before the subject; ich erwarte meinen Freund; daher muß ich zu Hause bleiben. Real conjunctions, which always stand at the beginning of a sentence, remove the copula to the end, such as, wenn, als, da, weil, nachdem, obgleich, obschon, obwohl, wenngleich, wiewohl, bevor, bis, dafern, damit, daß, ehe, falls, je, indem, ob, seitdem, sintemal, so bald, so lange, so weit, während, wie, wiefern, wofern. When secondary sentences, beginning with the following conjunctions, are put before the principal sentence; the latter generally begins with so: wenn, als, da, weil, nachdem, obgleich, obschon, obwohl, wenngleich, wennschon, wiewohl; as, als ich in London ankam, so fand ich meinen Freund nicht; when I arrived in London, I did not find my friend; weil Sie nicht zu Hause waren, so ging ich wieder fort, because you were not at home, I went away again. When, however, a secondary sentence stands after the copula of the principal sentence, it does not affect the order of the same; ich fand, als ich vor einigen Tagen in London ankam, meinen Freund nicht; er wird, so weit er kann, meinen Wunsch erfüllen. Examine the following

sentences : er war abgereiſet, ehe ich nach Paris kam; ehe ich nach Paris kam, war er abgereiſet ; ich weiß, daß er meinen Brief erhalten hat; daß er meinen Brief erhalten hat, weiß ich ; er will es nicht thun, weil er träge iſt; weil er träge iſt, ſo will er es nicht thun.

18. In sentences which begin with the above mentioned conjunctions, a personal pronoun may stand between the conjunction and the subject, this not being a personal pronoun itself : als ihn ſein Vater ſah, weinte dieſer vor Freuden.

19. The copula is also removed to the end of the sentence by the relative pronouns, welcher, der, was für ein, wer, was, and the relative adverbs or conjunctions, wo, warum, weßwegen, woher, wohin, &c. ; Der Mann, welcher mir den Brief brachte, hat mir die Nachricht mitgetheilt. Das Buch, welches ich vorige Woche las, fand ich ſehr unterhaltend. Dies iſt der Mann, deſſen Haus ich Ihnen dieſen Morgen zeigte. Ich werde mit Vergnügen thun, was mir befohlen worden iſt. Ich weiß nicht, wo ich ihn geſehen habe. Wer kann wiſſen, warum er nicht gekommen iſt ? Er ſagte mir nicht, was für ein Buch er mitgenommen habe.

20. When the sentence which begins with an indefinite relative pronoun, is put before the principal sentence, it removes the subject after the copula: Was mir befohlen worden iſt, werde ich mit Vergnügen thun. But when the subject is the same in both, the demonstrative pronouns der, das, are either not expressed or put before the copula : wer nicht hören will, muß fühlen, or, der muß fühlen. Was heute wahr iſt, muß auch morgen wahr ſeyn, or, das muß auch morgen wahr ſeyn.

21. In sentences, in which an auxiliary verb of moods, or such a verb as requires the infinitive without zu, occurs together with an infinitive, the copula does not stand at the end, but before the two infinitives. The close reiteration of werden in the future of the passive is,

likewise avoided by putting the copula before the participle or predicate: wenn ich es hätte thun müssen, so würde
ich es mit frohem Muthe gethan haben.   Obgleich ich ihn hatte
kommen hören, so konnte ich ihn doch im ganzen Hause nicht
finden.   Ich hoffe, daß alle Verleumbungen einst werden offenbar
werden.

22. In sentences with the perf. or pluperf. of the passive or the second future, or the second conditional of the
active or passive, the copula may stand before the participle or the predicate: niemand wird leugnen, daß die Uebel=
thäter hier auf Erden nicht immer sind bestraft worden, or
bestraft worden sind.   Sobald ich meinen Freund werde gesehen
haben, or gesehen haben werde, will ich Ihnen alles mittheilen.

23. Sentences in which a purpose or design is expressed by the infinitive mood with zu, or um zu, have
their natural place, like secondary sentences after the
subject of the principal sentence: der Sohn ist zehn Meilen
gegangen, um seinen Vater eine halbe Stunde zu sehen, or der
Sohn ist, um seinen Vater eine halbe Stunde zu sehen, zehn
Meilen gegangen, or um seinen Vater eine halbe Stunde zu
sehen, ist der Sohn zehn Meilen gegangen.

24. The five conjunctions: allein, denn, sondern, und,
and oder, always stand at the beginning of a sentence
without affecting the order of the words; aber and näm=
lich may stand at the beginning of a sentence, and in this
case they do not affect the order of the words; but they
may also stand after the copula and even after the object:
der Mann ist zwar reich; allein niemand achtet ihn, sondern
jedermann verachtet ihn; denn er ist ungerecht und geizig; aber
ich hoffe, (or ich hoffe aber) daß er sich bessern wird.

25. The following conjunctions have, like adverbs,
their place after the copula, and therefore remove the
subject after the copula when they are put at the beginning of the sentence or before the subject: doch, dennoch,

jeboch, zwar, indeffen, gleichwohl, daher, demnach, beffenungeachtet, defto, hingegen, außerdem, folglich, ferner, beßwegen, darum, nun, auch, nur, kaum, entweder, weder, noch.

26. But when the following conjunctions, auch, kaum, weder, noch, entweder, and the adverbs nur, sogar, schon, (sometimes also vielleicht and vermuthlich) have a particular reference to the subject, and not to the predicate, they do not affect the order of the words when they are put before the subject: nur der Mörder (or der Mörder nur) ist gehängt worden; aber nicht der Dieb. Auch mein Bruder hat es mir gesagt. Auch hat mein Bruder es mir gesagt. Kaum eine Stunde war vergangen. Kaum war eine Stunde vergangen. Schon drey Tage sind vergangen, und noch niemand ist erschienen.

27. The following conjunctions, doch, jedoch, indeffen, nun, and the adverbs, freylich, wahrlich, and some other adverbial expressions, such as, im Gegentheil, are sometimes employed elliptically, or as words of exclamation; in which case they do not affect the position of the subject: freylich, ich habe ihn selbst gesehen. Wahrlich, ich sage dir. Ich weiß noch nicht, ob ich es thun kann; doch, ich will mich besinnen.

I shall conclude this chapter with a few remarks on the position of adjectives and participles when employed in an attributive sense.

1. Adjectives, and words used as adjectives, such as participles, pronouns, and numerals, generally precede the substantive to which they belong, when they do not form the predicate. When adjectives and participles, used in the attributive sense, govern cases, the cases precede them; Ein gutes Haus; ein blühender Baum; ein liebender Vater; der geschriebene Brief; die zerstörte Stadt; ein langer Staab; ein schwerer Stein; ein würdiger Unterthan. Ein seine Kinder zärtlich liebender Vater. Der an meinen Vater geschriebene Brief. Die von den Soldaten zerstörte Stadt. Ein

zehn Ellen langer Staab. Ein zehn Pfund schwerer Stein. Ein der Ehre seines Fürsten würdiger Unterthan.

2. When a particular stress is to be laid on the adjective or participle, it is either put after the substantive like an apposition with the definite article, or a relative sentence is made of it; or it is used elliptically : Friedrich der zweyte; das Haus, das neue; der Eifer, auch der gute, kann verrathen. Der Führer, der blind ist, kann nicht leiten. Der Brief, geschrieben an meinen Vater. Die Stadt, von den Soldaten zerstört. Ein Vater, seine Kinder zärtlich liebend. Ein Mann, einer solchen Ehre würdig. In this elliptical manner, however, they can be used only when the substantive to which they belong is in the nominative or the accusative.

3. The present participle, when used elliptically, is preceded by the object which it governs : der Vater, seine Kinder zärtlich liebend; but the adjective and the preterite participle may stand before or after the object : der Mann, stolz auf seinen Reichthum, or, auf seinen Reichthum stolz; der Brief geschrieben an meinen Vater, or, an meinen Vater geschrieben; die Stadt, zerstört von den Soldaten, or, von den Soldaten zerstört. The preterite participle may even be put before the subject; in which case it removes the subject after the copula : Gewohnt den Gesetzgeber in Deutschland zu spielen, und selbst über das Schicksal des Kaisers zu gebieten, sah der stolze Churfürst von Baiern sich durch Wallensteins Erscheinung auf einmal entbehrlich gemacht.—(*Schiller's Thirty Years' War.*)

THE END.

J. Wertheimer & Co. Printers, Circus Place, Finsbury Circus.

EXERCISES

FOR

WRITING GERMAN,

ADAPTED TO THE RULES OF HIS

GERMAN GRAMMAR.

BY

THE REV. J. G. TIARKS, PH. DR.

MINISTER OF THE GERMAN PROTESTANT REFORMED CHURCH IN LONDON.

SECOND EDITION.

LONDON:

J. WACEY, 4, OLD BROAD-STREET; BLACK AND ARMSTRONG,
8, WELLINGTON-STREET, NORTH, STRAND; J. TAYLOR,
30, UPPER-GOWER-STREET; T. HURST,
ST. PAUL'S CHURCH-YARD.

W. GRAPEL, LIVERPOOL; J. WRIGHT, BRISTOL.

———

1837.

J. Wertheimer & Co. Printers, Circus Place, Finsbury Circus.

PREFACE.

THE first edition of these Exercises for Writing German, has been so favourably received by the public, that I have great pleasure in publishing a second one. Those who have used the first edition will perceive that I have made some alterations; but I hope that these alterations will be considered as improvements. I have arranged the notes in the second and third parts in the same way as in the Introductory Exercises, in order to enable the student to commit the single words in their original form to memory, before he commences the translation; and those who are anxious to secure all the advantages which may be derived from translating these Exercises, should never neglect doing so.

As I am not in the habit of using dialogues with my pupils, I have endeavoured to supply their place by introducing in these Exercises all the familiar phrases, generally found in dialogues ; and the student who takes the trouble of committing each exercise, after it has been corrected, to memory, will derive a double advantage from using these Exercises instead of dialogues. He will not only become familiar with all the common expressions of daily occurrence; but, at the same time, impress the grammatical forms of all the parts of speech, and the rules on the arrangement of words on his memory.

Experience has sufficiently proved that those who carefully translate and learn these Exercises, are thereby enabled to express themselves correctly in speaking, as well as in writing on common subjects.

Copies are prefixed for those who wish to learn the German hand-writing.

A key for self-tuition may be had.

JOH. GERH. TIARKS.

*67, Great Prescot Street, Goodman's-fields.
February 1837.*

** An Abstract of the Grammar, with Exercises ; for the Use of Schools, is in the Press.

German Handwriting.

A L L D C F G H

I J K L M N O P

Q R S T U V W X

Y Z

a b c d e f g h i

j k l m n o p q r

s s t u v w x y z

Double Letters

Ae ä, Oe ö, Ue ü.

st (st), ch (ch), ck (ck), ff (ff),

ss (ss), ß (ss), st (st), tz (tz).

meinen, deinen, keinen, seinen,

gehen, stehen, sehen, fliehen, drehen,

unten, munter, bunt, kund, gesund,

büßen, süß, Füße, Flüße, Grüße,

Hals, Hälfe, Gans, Gänse, Wand

Lust, Lüste, Stock, Stöcke, Floß,

Kiene, Leine, Keime, Leime,

Mund, Moos, Maaß, Mist, u. s. w.

Quelle, Feid, Putz, Zank, Zunft,

Namen Naturen, Katz, Nutzen,

Undank, Unsinn, Uebermaaß,

Antlitz, Ausländer, Aehnlichkeit,

Ofen, Dofen, Waßer, Wasser,

Leiden, London, Diener, Dämmerung

Ramen, Kamen, Summe, Zinn

wischen, wünschen, Volk, Vorl, von

Jesus ist gekommen!
Danket ihm, ihr Frommen
Dankt ihm daß er kam!
Daß er hier auf Erden,
Unser Heil zu werden
Eine Wohnung nahm.
Mensch wie wir,
Lebten er hier,
Um des Vaters gnäd'gen Willen
An uns zu erfüllen.

2.

Laßt uns niederfallen
Danken daß er Allen
Freund und Bruder ist!
Gott auf seinem Throne
Liebt uns in dem Sohne,
Hilft durch Jesum Christ.
Welch ein Heil,
An Christo Theil
Und durch seine Rettung Gaben
An Gott selbst zu haben.

Mein lieber Freund!

Sie würden mir einen großen Gefallen thun, wenn Sie den Mann zu mir schickten, welcher Ihnen ein schönes Pferd zu einem so billigen Preise anbot. Ich wünsche eins zu kaufen, und es ist nicht unwahrscheinlich, daß dasselbe mir gefallen wird. Kennen Sie es so wohl, daß Sie es in jeder Hinsicht empfehlen können? Da ich weiß, daß Sie ein so guter Kenner sind, so werde ich mich ganz nach Ihrem Urtheile richten. — Wenn ich Zeit habe, so komme ich diesen Abend zu Ihnen, um darüber mit Ihnen zu sprechen. Es that mir sehr leid zu hören, daß Sie nicht ganz wohl sagen.

Ich verbleibe mit Hochachtung u. Liebe
der Ihrige
A. P.

d. 2ten Februar,
1837

EXERCISES FOR WRITING GERMAN.

Haben, *to have.*

WE have a holiday. Have you pens? Thou hast money. I have an apple. Have they pears? He has flowers. I have had coffee, and he has had tea. Have you a bird? They have had paper, pens and ink. Hast thou had beer? We have had milk and water.

The holiday, ber Feiertag; the pen, bie Feber; the money, bas Gelb; the apple, ber Apfel; the pear, bie Birne; the flower, bie Blume; the coffee, ber Kaffee; the tea, ber Thee; the bird, ber Bogel; the paper, bas Papier; the ink, bie Dinte; the beer, bas Bier; the milk, bie Milch; the water, bas Waffer.

I had yesterday a holiday. Hadst thou a horse? He had a donkey. We shall have pleasure. He will have friends. She had had time. Will she have time? Will he have the books? Had we the knives, the forks and the spoons? Thou wilt have a garden. They will have grapes. You will have nothing. Had he had nothing? He will have had trouble. Shall we have had the pleasure?

The horse, bas Pferb; the donkey, ber Efel; the pleasure, bas Bergnügen; the friend, ber Freund; the time, bie Zeit; the book, bas Buch; the knife, bas Meffer; the fork, bie Gabel; the spoon, ber Löffel; the garden, ber Garten; the grape, bie Weintraube; nothing, nichts; the trouble, bie Mühe.

B

We should have had it. Have thou patience. Let him have patience. Let them have liberty. They would have success, if they had patience. If they had patience, they would have success. I should have had the book, if I had had money. If he had had money, he would have had a situation. We should have company, if we had time. Had she had money, she would have had friends.

Note. The conjunction wenn, *if*, throws the verb to the end of the sentence; and when the secondary sentence, which begins with *if*, is placed before the principal sentence, the subject of this sentence stands after the verb, and the sentence begins with *so*, in this manner, If they patience had, so would they success have.

It, es; the patience, die Gebuld; the liberty, die Freiheit; the success, das Glück; the book, das Buch; the money, das Geld; the situation, die Stelle; the company, die Gesellschaft; the time, die Zeit; the friend, der Freund; if, wenn.

Seyn, *to be*.

He is young, but she is old. I am happy, and they are unhappy. Are we contented? Yes. Are you poor? No, you are rich. He has been very ill. Has she been good? Are they white or black? They are neither white nor black, but green. Thou art not industrious. He has not been industrious. Has she been naughty? We have been honest. Have they been idle? Yes, very idle.

Young, jung; but, aber; old, alt; happy, glücklich; unhappy, unglücklich; contented, zufrieden; yes, ja; poor, arm; no, nein; rich, reich; very, sehr; ill, krank; good, gut; white, weiß; black, schwarz; neither—nor, weder—noch; but (after a negative) sondern; green, grün; industrious, fleißig; naughty, unartig; honest, ehrlich; idle, faul.

I was the friend of the boy. He was the son of a

merchant. Wast thou kind? No, thou wast not kind. Were you there? We had been very busy. It was quite right. How late was it? Was it not too late? I should have had it, if it had not been too late. They were dissatisfied. Why had they been dissatisfied? If I were rich, I should, perhaps, be learned. You were not so kind as he was. They had been very grateful.

The boy, ber Knabe; the son, ber Sohn; the merchant, ber Kaufmann; kind, gütig; not, nicht; there, da; busy, geschäftig; quite right, ganz recht; how, wie; late, spät; too, zu; dissatisfied, mißvergnügt; why, warum; rich, reich; perhaps, vielleicht, learned, gelehrt; so, so; grateful, bankbar.

He will soon be in London. Will he be the guide? I shall have been here an hour. You will be very tall. It will be early enough. We shall have been very angry. He would be clever, if he were attentive. If he were attentive, he would be clever. I should have been a fool, if I had been so careless. Be so kind, my friend. Let it be so. We shall be sincere. Should we have been his enemy? Let us always be faithful It would have been better, if we had not had it. She would be amiable, if she were not so talkative.

Soon, bald; the guide, ber Führer; here, hier; the hour, bie Stunde; tall, groß; early enough, früh genug; angry, zornig, böse; clever, geschickt; attentive, aufmerksam; the fool, ber Thor; careless, nachlässig; sincere, aufrichtig; the enemy, ber Feind; always, immer; better, besser; amiable, liebenswürdig; talkative, geschwätzig.

Werben, to become.

He has become rich. I shall become wise. They became suddenly ill. Have they become too weak? I should have become his friend, if I had become acquainted with him. It is getting late. They got tired

and sleepy. The children grow very tall. The trees
have become green. Do not become impatient. Didst
thou become troublesome?

Rich, reich; wise, weise; suddenly, plötzlich; weak, schwach;
acquainted, bekannt; with, mit, (gov. the dative), tired, müde;
sleepy, schläfrig; the tree, der Baum; impatient, ungeduldig;
troublesome, lästig.

ON THE DECLENSION OF SUBSTANTIVES.

The virtue of the man is great. The leaves of the
tree are green. He is the master of the house. The
colour of the ink is black. We love the boy. I
praise the industry of the boys. The hope of the
father is the wish of the mother. We cut with a knife;
we write with a pen; we dig with a spade; we eat with
a spoon; we see with our eyes; we hear with our ears;
we smell with our nose. The books are on (auf) the
table. The tables are in the room. The birds are on
the roof of the house. The windows of the houses are
large. I give the apples to the children. We wish
our friend success. I do not know the sister of my
friend.

The leaf, das Blatt; the master, der Herr; to love, lieben;
to praise, loben; the industry, der Fleiß; the wish, der Wunsch;
to cut, schneiden; to write, schreiben; to dig, graben; the spade,
der Spaten; to eat, essen; to see, sehen; the eye, das Auge; to
hear, hören; the ear, das Ohr; to smell, riechen; the nose, die
Nase; the room, das Zimmer; the roof, das Dach; the window,
das Fenster; success, Glück; to know, kennen.

The value of gold and silver is great. The value
of iron and copper is not so great. The song of birds
is sweet. The children stand at (an, with the dative)
the door. The glasses are on the table. The life of
men on earth is short. We are on (an, dat.) the brink

of the grave. The utility of horses, cows, sheep and geese, is great. We love the virtues of the women, and we admire the beauties of nature. I am grateful for (für, acc.) the health of my body. He is acquainted with the arts and sciences. God knows the thoughts of men. He sends messengers to (zu, dat.) the king and the queen. The feet of the messengers of peace are welcome. The ships are in a haven. He fought with the courage of a lion.

Note. The definite article must be used in German before substantives which represent a whole species.

The value, der Werth; the iron, das Eisen; the copper, das Kupfer; the song, der Gesang; sweet, süß; to stand, stehen; the door, die Thüre; the-glass, das Glas; the life, das Leben; the earth, die Erde; short, kurz; the brink, der Rand; the grave, das Grab; the utility, der Nutzen; the horse, das Pferd; the cow, die Kuh; the sheep, das Schaaf; the goose, die Gans; to admire, bewundern; the beauty, die Schönheit; grateful, dankbar; the health, die Gesundheit; the body, der Leib; acquainted, bekannt; the art, die Kunst; the science, die Wissenschaft; to know, kennen; the thought, der Gedanke; to send, schicken; the messenger, der Bothe; the foot, der Fuß; welcome, willkommen; the ship, das Schiff; the haven, der Hafen; to fight, kämpfen; the courage, der Muth; the lion, der Löwe.

ON THE DECLENSION OF ADJECTIVES.

The man is ignorant. He is an ignorant man. The pride of an ignorant man is often great. We are weak. We are weak creatures. Man is a weak creature. The good father of the poor boy has great patience. In the beautiful garden of the kind woman, are blue and yellow flowers. We had sweet apples, pears, and cherries. The sweet apples are better than the sweet pears. A sour apple is unwholesome. I have bought a beautiful garden for my dear children. They live in a large house. This little child has a kind heart and a sound understanding. A long passage leads to (nach, dat.) a deep well.

Ignorant, unwiffend; the pride, der Stolz; weak, schwach; the creature, das Geschöpf; the patience, die Geduld; kind, gütig; blue, blau; yellow, gelb; sweet, süß; the cherry, die Kirsche; sour, sauer; unwholesome, ungesund; to buy, kaufen; to live, wohnen; sound, gesund; the understanding, der Verstand; the passage, der Gang; to lead, führen; deep, tief; the well, der Brunnen.

There (es) lived once a poor woman in a large town of a distant land; and she had in the whole world not a single enemy. We see beautiful shops in the long streets of this great metropolis. I shall do it with great pleasure. Evident proofs of a noble heart afford great pleasure. We have had clear days but dark nights. We cannot see the numberless stars in the dark nights. London is not an unhealthy place. They live in (an, dat.) an unhealthy place. A modest man says nothing impertinent to a modest man. We could do it under these favorable ' circumstances. Favorable circumstances induce me to do it. It was a favorable circumstance.

Once, einmal; distant, fern; whole, ganz; the enemy, der Feind; the shop, der Laden; the street, die Straße; the metropolis, die Hauptstadt; evident, deutlich; the proof, der Beweis; to afford, gewähren; clear, hell; dark, dunkel; numberless, zahllos; the star, der Stern; unhealthy, ungesund; the place, der Ort; modest, bescheiden; impertinent, unbescheiden; favorable, günstig; the circumstance, der Umstand; to induce, bewegen.

ON THE COMPARISON OF ADJECTIVES.

The days are now longer than the nights. The nights are longest in winter. The longest life of a man is short. I expected a larger company. My friend

lives in a larger and more beautiful house than I. The
inhabitants of the most beautiful houses are not always
happy. He is the happiest man. William is a more
industrious boy than Henry; but Francis is the most
industrious boy in the school. John was to-day more
industrious than yesterday; but he will be most industrious to-morrow. He is the kindest father. You
are the son of the kindest father. It is best. It is
newest. We are richest, when we are most contented.

Now, jeßt; than, als; the night, bie Nacht; short, kurz; to
expect, erwarten; large, groß; the company, bie Gesellschaft;
beautiful, schön; the inhabitant, ber Einwohner; always, immer;
happy, glücklich; William, Wilhelm; industrious, fleißig; Henry,
Heinrich; Francis, Franz; the school, bie Schule; John, Johann;
to-day, heute; yesterday, gestern; to-morrow, morgen; kind,
gütig; new, neu; rich, reich; contented, zufrieden.

ON THE CARDINAL AND ORDINAL NUMBERS.

How old is the son of the woman? Twelve years.
How long have you lived in this street? Ten years, four
months, and five days. To-day is the sixth of Decem-
ber. On (an, dat.) the seventeenth of August I shall
be eighteen years old. Edward the Sixth was the son
of Henry the Eighth. I have sent five and twenty
letters to (auf, acc.) the post. In the year one thousand
eight hundred and thirty-seven I shall make a journey.
Four hundred and seventy-nine English miles are about
ninety-five German miles.

How, wie; long, lange, to live, wohnen; the month, ber
Monat, Edward, Eduard; to send, schicken; the post, bie Post;
to make, machen; a journey, eine Reise; English, Englisch; the
mile, bie Meile; about, ohngefähr.

meinen, deinen, keinen, seinen;

gehen, stehen, sehen, flehen, drehen;

unten, munter, bunt, kund, gesund;

büßen, süß, Süße, Flüsse, Güsse,

Hals, Hälfte, Gans, Gänse, Rand

Brust, Brüste, Stock, Stöcke, Roß,

Hein, Leine, Keime, Leime;

Mund, Moos, Maaß, Mist; u.s.w.

Quelle, Heil, Putz, Zank, Zunft,

Namen Naturen, Katz, Nutzen,

Undank, Unsinn, Uebermaaß,

Antlitz, Andenken, Aehnlichkeit,

Ofen, Dofen; Waster, Masken,

Laiden, London; Dinner, Dämmerung

Rammen, Kommen, Summe; Zinn

wischen, wünschen, Volk, Verb. von

The sister, die Schwester; the wife, die Frau, or die Gemah-linn; the cousin, der Vetter; to lose, verlieren (irr.); the purse, der Beutel; to sell, verkaufen; the neighbour, der Nachbar; to write, schreiben; to know, wissen; the cause, die Ursache; the misfortune, das Unglück; to grieve, betrüben; the pencil, die Bleifeder; the inkstand, das Tintenfaß; the slate, die Rechen-tafel; the drawing, die Zeichnung.

ON THE DEMONSTRATIVE PRONOUNS.

This knife is sharper than that. The colour of this cloth is green. I cannot write with this pen. Do you see that bird? He lives in that house. I am acquainted with that circumstance. These virtues are rare. Those boys are my sons. Have you spoken to (mit, dat.) those girls? The objects of art are beautiful, but those of nature are more beautiful. The garden of my friend is small, but that of my neighbour is smaller. I have seen the portrait of the king, and also that of the queen. Do you know that? I do not remember that. I bought that book, which you saw. I bought it of that man whom you recommended.

Note. The relative pronoun removes the verb to the end of the sentence.

Sharp, scharf; the cloth, das Tuch; acquainted, bekannt; the circumstance, der Umstand; rare, selten; to speak, sprechen; the object, der Gegenstand; the art, die Kunst; the portrait, das Bildniß; to remember, sich erinnern (gov. the gen. case); to re-commend, empfehlen (irr.)

He who stands in that corner is my father. I spoke of (von, dat.) him who stands at (an, dat.) the door. Do you know her, who sits in the arm-chair? It is the same face. I come with the same request. You will find the same difficulties. That man who is cruel, cannot be good. That woman who has many children has much to do. Those children who have a kind

father are fortunate. The happiness of that man who
fears God, is greater than the happiness of him who
lives without God in this world. This is a cock, but
that is a hen. These are strawberries, and those are
raspberries.

To stand, ſtehen; the corner, bie Ecke; to speak, ſprechen (irr.);
the door, bie Thür; to know, kennen; to sit, ſitzen; the armchair,
ber Lehnſtuhl; the face, bas Geſicht; to come, kommen; the request, bie Bitte; to find, finben; the difficulty, bie Schwierigkeit;
cruel, grauſam; many, viele; much, viel; to do, thun; fortunate, glücklich; the happiness, bie Glückſeligkeit; to fear, fürchten;
to live, leben; without, ohne; the world, bie Welt; the cock,
ber Hahn; the hen, bie Henne; the strawberry, bie Erbbeere;
the raspberry, bie Himbeere.

ON THE RELATIVE AND INTERROGATIVE PRONOUNS.

The man, who sold me the horse, is dead. The man,
whose horse I bought, is still alive. The boy, to whom
I gave the money, is the son of our gardener: He has
lost the money which I gave him. The apples which ~
you sent me, are very fine. We call that heavenly
body the brightness of which our eyes cannot bear, the
sun. The chair, on (auf, dat.) which I am sitting, is
too high. The virtues which she possesses, make her
dear to us. Those who are richest are not always
happiest. Charity, the practice of which is our duty,
makes us happy. That is a circumstance, with which
I am not acquainted. Do not forget the subjects on
(über, acc.) which I have spoken to (mit, dat.) you.

N. B. The gen. of the relative *which* always stands before the
word which governs it; say: of which brightness, for, the brightness of which; and use the gen. of ber.

To sell, verkaufen; dead, tobt; still, noch; alive, am Leben;
to give, geben (irr.); the gardener, ber Gärtner; to lose, verlieren (irr.); to send, ſchicken; the heavenly body, ber Himmels-

Körper; the brightness, der Glanz; to bear, ertragen; the chair, der Stuhl; high, hoch; to possess, besitzen; dear, lieb; charity, die Liebe; the practice, die Uebung; the duty, die Pflicht; the circumstance, der Umstand; acquainted, bekannt; to forget, vergessen (irr.); the subject, der Gegenstand.

Who is in the room? Whose book is this? Whom did you send? To whom did you pay the money? Who has done this? I cannot tell you, who has done it. Which of these boys has been naughty? Can you tell me which of these boys has been naughty? What did he say? I do not know what he said. Whose pens have you taken? To whom do you speak? It was this child to whom I spoke. Who are these men? He who is contented is rich. I know all that he said. I gave you all that I had. I know what has happened. He who talks much, does little. Which are the books? Who could know that? The man who could know it is absent. We who could know it, were not asked. Do you know my friend B, whom I showed you yesterday?

Note 1. Ascertain first whether the relative pronoun is *definite*, or *indefinite.* The definite relative pronoun is: welcher, welche, welches, instead of which also the demonstrative, der, die, das, is used. The indefinite is, wer, was. This is so indefinite, that it has neither feminine gender nor plur. number.

Note 2. The interrogative pronoun does not remove the verb to the end of the sentence, like the relative. Therefore ascertain first, whether the pronoun is used as an interrogative or a relative. In the sentence: who has done this, *who*, is an interrogative, and the order of the words is: who has this done; but in the following: I cannot tell you who has done it, *who* is a relative, and the order of the words is: I can you not tell, who it done has. The last sentence is called in the German Latin, and Greek grammars, an indirect question.

The room, das Zimmer; to pay, bezahlen; to do, thun, *part.* gethan; to tell, sagen; naughty, unartig; to know, wissen, *french,* savoir; kennen, *french*, connoitre. Wiffen is used of notions which we comprehend with our mind; kennen, of objects and notions with which we are only acquainted; as: ich weiß ben Namen des Mannes; ich kenne ben Mann; to take, nehmen (irr.); contented, zufrieben; to happen, geschehen; it has happened, es ist geschehen; to talk, sprechen; absent, abwesenb; to ask, fragen; to show, zeigen.

ON THE AUXILIARY VERBS OF MOODS.

We may not do it. He has not liked (mögen) to do it. May I see what you are doing? Your friend would not do me the favor. His father has not been willing (perf. of wollen) to give him a horse. I will not quarrel with you. Tell the boy that he shall have it soon. The door ought to be opened now. Your sister ought to have kept her promise. Can you tell me who lives in that house? The merchant could not pay his debts. He has not been able to get the book. Had he been able to get it, he would have bought it with pleasure. His children are not allowed (pres. of bürfen) to play with mine. Why have the children not been allowed to play? Why has he not done it? He has not been allowed. The man must be in bad circumstances. My servant was obliged (müffen) to wait a whole hour. Our master has been obliged to punish two boys. Let me do it. He made him go out of (aus, dat.) the house.

Note. As the verbs, *may, will, shall, ought, can, must*, have neither an infinitive nor a preterite participle, the perf. pluperf. and future tenses cannot be formed; and when these tenses are required, we must have recourse to other verbs; as, I can do it; I could do it; I have been able to do it; I must do it; I have been obliged to do it. But we have no synonymous verb for *ought ;* and therefore the perf. and pluperf. tenses are expressed by putting the auxiliary *to have*, before the infinitive of the verb which *ought* modifies; as, I ought to have done it; id) ꜧätte eß tꜧun ſollen. Jd) ꜧätte eß tꜧun mögen, is not expressed by, I liked to have done it, but by, I should have liked to do it.

The favour, ber Gefallen; to quarrel, zanꜧen; to open, öffnen; soon, balb; now, jeꜧt; to keep, ꜧalten; the promise, baß Berſprecꜧen; the merchant, ber Kaufmann; to pay, bezaꜧlen; the debt, ber Sdulb; to get, beꜧommen; to play, ſpielen; bad, ſcꜧlecꜧt; the servant, ber Diener; to wait, warten; the master, ber Leꜧrer; to punish, beſtrafen.

We have not been able to read his letter. They have not been willing to do me that favour. He has been obliged to confess it. I ought to have written to (an, acc.) my sister. Ye have not been allowed to drink wine. We have not liked (mögen) to drink water. He will be able to do it to-morrow. My neighbour is said to be rich. It may (ꜧönnen) be; but we must not believe all that (waß) people say. How long have you been obliged to wait? You will never be able to finish this work. I shall never like to travel by night.

To read, leſen; the letter, ber Brief; to confess, beꜧennen; to drink, trinꜧen; to believe, glauben; people, bie Leute; how, wie; never, niemalß; to finish, beenbigen; the work, baß Werꜧ; to travel, reiſen; by night, in ber Nacꜧt, or beß Nacꜧtß.

ON THE IRREGULAR VERBS.

Your father has not given me the answer which I expected. Have you read the history of the Reformation? Who has written the history of the Crusades which you lent me? It was ten o'clock when I came home. You ought not to have eaten and drunk so much. The boy sat on (auf, dat.) a chair, and his mother stood by him. Your son has brought me your letter; I thought he had lost it. If I had known that you knew this man, I should have sent him to (zu, dat.) you. We have spokeu to (mit, dat.) him on (über, acc.)

the subject. Is your father at home? No; he is gone
to (nach, dat.) town. Give (2nd per. sing.) me a sheet
of paper and two pens. Read this sentence once more.
Do not speak to him. My friend has not suffered much;
he died on the tenth of July. "The apple does not fall
far from the stem," is a German proverb. Where is
my hat? It hangs on that nail. Where is Henry? He
is washing his hands. Francis is reading the newspaper.

The answer, der Antwort; to expect, erwarten; to read, lefen;
the history, der Gefchichte; the Reformation, der Reformation;
the Crusades, die Kreuzzüge; to lend, leihen; home, nach
Haufe; to eat, effen; to drink, trinken; to sit, fitzen; to stand,
ftehen; to lose, verlieren; to speak, fprechen; the subject, der
Gegenftand; at home, zu Haufe; to go, gehen; the sentence, der
Satz; once more, noch einmal; to suffer, leiden; to die, fterben;
to fall, fallen; the stem, der Stamm; the proverb, das Sprich=
wort; the hat, der Hut; to hang, hangen; the nail, der Nagel;
to wash, wafchen; the newspaper, die Zeitung.

ON THE COMPOUND VERBS.

First Class (separable.)

We copy his letters. This boy has copied his translation. Will you copy this for me? The mail arrives
at (um) seven o'clock. The mail has not yet arrived.
The moon rose this evening at nine o'clock. Why
have you given it up? Do not give it up. Where is
your mother? She is gone out. At (um. acc.) what
time did she go out? At ten o'clock. Will you listen
to me? I will read my letter to you. Has he read the
passage to you? Read this passage once more to me.
Take your slate away. I shall take it away very soon.
Why have you taken my hat away? Do not prefer
money to virtue. Cato preferred death to captivity. I

should not have preferred his company to yours. The ambassador has been recalled. The plan has been given up. The vessel is sunk, and ten men have perished. I wish to go out; but I cannot. I had no time to copy my letter. We were compelled to give it up.

To copy, abſchreiben; the translation, bie Ueberſeҫung; the mail, bie Poſt; to arrive, anfommen; to rise, aufgeҫen; to give up, aufgeben; to go out, ausgeben; to listen to, zuҫören (gov. dat.); to read to, vorleſen (gov. dat.); the passage, bie Stelle; once more, noch einmal; to take away, wegnehmen; the slate, bie Rechentafel; to prefer, vorziehen; the death, ber Tob; the captivity, bie Gefangenſchaft; the company, bie Geſellſchaft; the ambassador, ber Geſanbte; to recall, zurücrufen; the plan, ber Plan; to give up, aufgeben; the vessel, bas Schiff; to sink, finfen (irr.); to perish, umfommen; to compel, zwingen (irr.)

SECOND CLASS (inseparable).

We commit a sin when we speak an untruth. Many sins are committed in order to obtain money. A new machine has been invented. Can you tell me who has invented it? We do not always attain our object. Do you understand me? I do not understand every word. I have been misled by the outward appearance. Two mistakes have escaped my attention. Whoever commits a crime dishonors himself. The whole town has been destroyed. My dear boy, you have misunderstood me. What you have done displeases me much. My friend has left a large fortune. Why did you not resist the temptation? Do not trouble yourself, I shall answer the letter. Can you explain this sentence to me? I have often explained it, and I hope that I shall be able to explain it to you. Your mother has spoiled you entirely. I will excuse you this time.

To commit, begehen; the sin, bie Sünbe; to speak, reben; in order to, um—zu; the machine, bie Maſchine; to invent, erfinben;

to attain, erreichen; the object, der Zweck; to understand, verstehen; to mislead, verführen; the outward appearance, der äußere Schein; the mistake, der Fehler; to escape, entgehen; the attention, die Aufmerksamkeit; the crime, das Verbrechen; to dishonor, entehren; to destroy, zerstören; to misunderstand, mißverstehen; to displease, mißfallen; much, sehr; to leave, hinterlassen; the fortune, das Vermögen; to resist, widerstehen (gov. dat.); the temptation, die Versuchung; to trouble, bemühen; to answer, beantworten; to explain, erklären; the sentence, der Satz; to spoil, verwöhnen; entirely, gänzlich.

ON THE ARRANGEMENT OF WORDS.

Rule 1—4. The grass is green. The boys write. Man is a mortal creature. He can write. We go out. I have been imprudent. The children would have been wiser. I ought to have spoken. I have been able to work. My mother would have been blamed. They are gone out. We have been obliged to wait.

The grass, das Gras; mortal, sterblich; the creature, das Geschöpf; imprudent, unvorsichtig; wise, weise; to blame, tabeln; to be obliged, müssen; to wait, warten.

Rule 5—8. The child has made a mistake. Many children make mistakes. We encourage our friends. Our friends have encouraged us. We are grateful to our friends. They begin their work. They have accomplished their work. The father can give his son no hope. The master has given the servant his wages. The son will relate the story to his father. The judge has given up the criminal to the gaoler. My neighbour will introduce your son to his friend. He has given it to me. He has recommended me to you. I shall send you the books. I shall give them to you.

The mistake, der Fehler; to encourage, aufmuntern; grateful, dankbar; to begin, anfangen; the work, die Arbeit; to accomplish, zu Stande bringen; the master, der Herr; the servant, ber Diener; the wages, ber Lohn; the judge, ber Richter; to give up, übergeben; the criminal, ber Verbrecher; the gaoler, ber Kerkermeister; to introduce, vorstellen.

Rule 9—13. You have written this page carelessly. This man writes his letters carelessly. Your friend has treated my son kindly. I have heard the account with great pleasure. I shall write to-morrow a long letter to my mother. You shall not play at cards on a Sunday. I saw him the day before yesterday. The master of this house died four days ago at Paris. We shall see you this afternoon at four o'clock at (in dat.) our house. I have found the book on the table. I shall send a parcel to Germany next week. Our gardener found yesterday a beautiful flower in our garden. Your brother did not give me the money yesterday, but the day before yesterday. He did not give me a pen, but a pencil. He did not do it yesterday, but the day before yesterday. We have seen the gentleman at church. We shall receive no news from them. You have, perhaps, misunderstood the child.

The page, bie Seite; carelessly, nachlässig; to treat, behandeln; kindly, gütig; the account, bie Nachricht; to play at cards, Karten spielen; the day before yesterday, vorgestern; the master, ber Herr; to die, sterben (irr.); the parcel, bas Packet; the gentleman, ber Herr; at church, in ber Kirche; to receive, erhalten; news, Neuigkeiten; to misunderstand, mißverstehen.

Rule 14. My brother will, with pleasure, send you to-morrow his horse. I could not give him yesterday the wished for answer.

N.B. The words of these two sentences are first to be put in their proper order; and then to be transposed according to rule.

Wished for, gewünscht; the answer, bie Antwort.

Rule 15—18. Do not speak to him. Should the tailor come, he must wait. If you will wait an hour, I

will go with you. I will go with you, if you will wait
an hour. When (als) the sun rose, the fog disap-
peared. As (ba) I am not well, I shall stay at home
to-day. Although he is rich, yet he is not happy.
After we had worked ten hours, we were very tired.
I told him that you could not come to-day. We shall
go home before it gets dark. I shall keep the horse
until you pay the money. Whilst we were walking, he
related to me his history. My father will grant your
request as far as he can do it.

The tailor, der Schneider; to rise, aufgehen; the fog, der
Nebel; to stay at home, zu Hause bleiben; tired, müde; it gets
dark, es wird finster; to keep, behalten; to walk, spazieren; to
grant, gewähren; the request, die Bitte.

Rule 19—23. The town which they have built, is
very small. Can you tell me where this man lives?
Can you tell me why he has done this? I do not know
whither he is gone. I cannot tell you who has given
me the information. What I have written, I have
written. Who is not for (für, acc.) us, is against
(wider, acc.) us. If I had been able to do it, I should
have done it. I know that the wicked will once be
punished. I went this morning to him, in order to deliver the letter which I had received. In order to learn
the conditions, I wrote him a letter.

The town, die Stadt; to build, bauen; whither, wohin; the
information, die Nachricht; I am able, ich kann; the wicked, die
Bösen; to punish, bestrafen; once, einst; in order to, um—zu;
to deliver, überliefern; to receive, erhalten; to learn, erfahren;
the condition, die Bedingung.

Rule 24—27. He has, indeed, worked long, but he
has done little. We must praise him, for he has acted
well. He has not only been industrious, but also made
progress. I have requested him to pay me the money,

but he will not do it. Scarcely an hour had passed, when he came to my house. He will neither convince me nor him. He must either return the book, or send me the money.

Indeed, zwar; to act, handeln; industrious, fleißig; progress, Fortschritte; to request, bitten; to pay, bezahlen; scarcely, kaum; it has passed, es ist vergangen; neither—nor, weder—noch; to convince, überzeugen; either—or, entweder—oder; to return, zurückschicken.

I have often praised this man, and I shall praise him now, for I know that he deserves praise. If he deserved blame, I should blame him, although he is my friend; for I will not be partial, but impartial. I am not yet tired, although I have worked eight hours. Although I have worked eight hours, I am not yet tired. If the horse which I bought of (von, dat.) you, had been stronger, I should not have sold it. I should not have sold the horse which I bought of you, if it had been stronger. Had the horse which I bought of you, been stronger, I should not have sold it. You know that we love these children. That we love these children, you know. We shall not go out to-day, because it is too cold. It is too cold; therefore we shall not go out to-day.

To deserve, verdienen; praise, Lob; blame, Tadel; to blame, tadeln; partial, partheyisch; not yet, noch nicht; tired, müde; strong, stark; to sell, verkaufen; to go out, ausgehen.

ON SOME PREPOSITIONS.

Wegen, on account of (gen.); während, (gen.) during; um—willen, (gen.) for the sake of; anstatt, (gen.) instead of; aus, out of, from (dat.); bey, with, near, on (dat.); mit, with (dat.); nach, after, to (dat.); seit, since (dat.); von, from, of, by (dat.); zu, to, at (dat.)

Have you spoken to him on account of the books?
We have not seen her since the death of her child. Is
your father at home? No, he went this moment out of
the house; I believe he is gone to your house. Has
any body been here during my absence? No, nobody.
Will you have the goodness to send this parcel to my
house? With the greatest pleasure. We intend to leave
London on account of the health of our children. When
did you hear from your father and mother? I heard
yesterday from them; I had a letter from my mother;
she mentioned that my aunt was with her. I must do
it for the sake of my honour. We shall be with you at
the appointed hour. Will you take a walk with me
after (the) tea? I come, instead of my father. When
did you return from your journey? Two days after your
departure.

The moment, der Augenblick; to believe, glauben; any body,
jemand; the absence, die Abwesenheit; the goodness, die Güte;
the parcel, das Packet; to intend, gedenken; to leave, verlassen;
the health, die Gesundheit; to mention, erwähnen; the aunt, die
Tante; appointed, bestimmt; to take a walk, einen Spaziergang
machen; to return, zurückkehren; the departure, die Abreise.

Durch, through, by (acc.); für, for (acc.); ohne, without (acc.);
gegen, towards, against (acc.); um, (acc.) around, about, at;
an, on, near, at (dat. and acc.); auf, on, (dat. and acc.); in, in,
into (dat. and acc.); über, over, above, beyond, on (dat. and
acc.); unter, under, beneath, among (dat. and acc.); vor, before,
ago (dat. and acc.); zwischen, between (dat. and acc.); hinter,
behind (dat. and acc.)

The inundation was so great, that the water flowed
through the houses which stood on the bank of the
river. Many children fell into the water, but they crept
out without the assistance of their parents. Your son
refused to assist me, in this affair; he will do nothing
for me, although I have always been very kind towards

him. The children were standing around the table when I came into the room. Much may happen in the course of a year. A naked sword hung over his head whilst he was sitting on his throne. I would not advise you to walk over this bridge. It rained two hours ago, and now it freezes. We have a large field behind our garden. There is no passage between these two houses. Why did you not put the money on the table? There was no room on the table. Where is your daughter? You will find her among those girls. I am much obliged to you for your kindness. You would do me a great favour, if you would speak to your friend on the subject.

The inundation, bie Ueberſchwemmung; to flow, fließen, irr.; the bank, bas Ufer; to fall, fallen, irr.; to creep out, heraus= kriechen, irr.; the parents, bie Eltern; to refuse, ſich weigern; the affair, bie Angelegenheit; to happen, geſchehen; the course, ber Lauf; naked, bloß; the sword, bas Schwerbt; to hang, hangen, irr.; whilst, während; to sit, ſiken, irr.; the throne, ber Thron; advise, rathen, (gov. dat.); the bridge, bie Brücke; the passage, ber Gang; to put, legen; the room, ber Raum, ber Plak; the favour, ber Gefallen; the subject, ber Gegenſtanb.

ON SOME CONJUNCTIONS.

Aber, but; ſonbern, but; baß, that; bamit, in order that; als, when; wenn, when, if; ba, as; inbem, since; ſeitbem, since; nachbem, after; weil, because; obgleich, although; je—beſto, the—the.

I shall not go out to-day, since I am not well. I have been very unwell since you were here, but I hope that I shall soon be well again. You are not poor, but rich; if you really were poor, I should do for you what I can. The more we do for this man, the more he expects. I cannot yet tell you when I shall have time to copy the two letters. Although I have a great wish to

do it, yet I am afraid that several circumstances will
prevent me. Examine the things well, in order. that
you may not be deceived. As it is so .very cold, I do
not expect to see my sister to-night. She did not come
yesterday, because it was too cold. When I walk fast,
I soon get warm; even if the weather is very cold.
We were richly rewarded, after we had suffered much.
You ought to have been here not at two, but at three
o'clock. The longer· the days are, the shorter are the
nights. When they returned from their journey, I found
them so altered, that I did not know them.

Really, wirflich; to expect, erwarten; to tell, sagen; to copy,
abschreiben; I am afraid, ich befürchte; to prevent, verhindern;
to examine, untersuchen; the things, die Sachen; to deceive,
betrügen, irr.; to-night, diesen Abend; to walk, gehen; fast,
schnell; richly, reichlich; to reward, belohnen; to suffer,
leiden, irr.; altered, verändert.

Daher, therefore; darum, on that account, for that reason;
dennoch, nevertheless; doch, yet, still; endlich, at length; hernach
and nachher, afterwards; jedoch, yet, however; nicht allein, nicht
nur, nicht bloß, not only; sondern auch, but also; so—auch,
however; so wohl—als auch, as well as, both—and; neither—nor,
weder—noch; entweder—oder, either—or; zwar, indeed, it is
true.

The boy could not find the gentleman to whom you
sent him with a letter; he therefore brought it back.
We expect to-night some friends; for that reason we
must stay at home. This man has been in my service,
and nevertheless he maintains that he does not know
me. However rich he is, yet he is not happy. Both
his father and his uncle advised him to have nothing to
do with this man; but he would not listen to (auf, acc.)
their advice. I esteem him for (wegen) his piety as
well as for his learning. At length, my dear friend, I
have not only received your letter, but also the parcel,

which you sent me. I cannot show you my garden now, I will do it afterwards. At first he refused to pay me the money, but afterwards he did it. You have either misunderstood me, or acted against my will. I can tell you, that you will neither see him, nor hear from him. He has, indeed, promised you to return, but I know that he will not keep his promise.

To bring back, jurückbringen; the service, der Dienst; to maintain, behaupten; the uncle, der Oheim; to advise, rathen; to listen, hören; to esteem, achten; the piety, die Frömmigkeit; the learning, die Gelehrsamkeit; at first, anfangs; to misunderstand, mißverstehen; to promise, versprechen, irr.; to return, zurückkehren; the promise, das Versprechen.

GENERAL SENTENCES.

How do you do, my dear friend? I thank you, I am pretty well now. Last week I had a very bad cold. The weather has been extremely cold. Where have you been the whole morning? I have been on the ice; I am very fond of skating. If you had told me that you intended to go, I should have gone with you. To-morrow you must not go without me. How do you like England? I like it very well, but I hope I shall like it still better in a few years. How long have you been here? About nine months. Could you speak English, when you arrived in London? Not a word. Then you have made rapid progress. The knowledge of Latin was of great use to me. Do you find the English language difficult? The pronunciation I find very difficult. I wish to see Mr. N—; can you tell me where he lives, and at what time I shall most probably find him at home? If I am not mistaken, he lives in the Strand; and, if you go at ten o'clock, you will

be sure to find him at home.   If I had time, I should
go with you.   Can you recommend me a good book-
seller ? If you wish to buy German books, I advise you
to go to Mr. Wacey, near the Royal Exchange, or to
Messrs. Black and Armstrong, No. 8, Wellington-street,
North, Strand.

A cold, *eine Erkältung*; the ice, *das Eis*; to be very fond of
a thing, *ein großer Freund von etwas seyn*; to skate, *Schlittschuh
laufen*, irr.; I like, *mir gefällt*; about, *ohngefähr*; to arrive,
ankommen, irr.; rapid, *schnell*; progress, *Fortschritte*; the knowledge, *die Kenntniß*; Latin, *das Lateinische*; the pronunciation,
die Aussprache; probably, *wahrscheinlich*; I am mistaken, *ich irre
mich*; the Strand, *der Strand*; you are sure to find him, *Sie
finden ihn gewiß*; to recommend, *empfehlen*, irr.; near, *nahe
bey*; the Royal Exchange, *die Königliche Börse*; Mr. *Herr*,
Messrs. *Herren*.

Will you have the goodness to awake me, for I wish
to rise early.   Why do you wish to rise early ? Do you
intend to go out ? No, I have some letters to write.
Will you dine with me to-morrow ? With great pleasure.   At what time do you dine ? At five o'clock.
May I offer you some roast beef ? Yes, I thank you.
Mutton is much better in England than in Germany.
Do you like roast pork ? I like it very much.   Will you
allow me to give you a potatoe ? No, I thank you, I
shall take some peas.   Do you not eat mustard with
your roast beef ? Yes, I like the English mustard very
much.

To awake, *wecken*; to rise, *aufstehen*; early, *früh*; to dine, *zu
Mittag essen*; to offer, *anbieten*; roast beef, *gebratenes Rind-
fleisch*; mutton, *Hammelfleisch*; I like, *ich mag*; I like much, *ich
mag gern*; the potatoe, *die Kartoffel*; the pea, *die Erbse*;
the mustard, *der Senf*.

J. Wertheimer & Co. Printers, Circus Place, Finsbury Circus.

School Books,

PUBLISHED

BY J. SOUTER,

SCHOOL LIBRARY, 131, FLEET STREET,

(REMOVED FROM ST. PAUL'S CHURCH-YARD,)

LONDON.

WHERE MAY BE HAD ALL OTHER

SCHOOL-BOOKS, COPYBOOKS, SLATES, PENCILS, PENS, AND ALL KINDS OF STATIONERY,

ON THE MOST REASONABLE TERMS.

.·. SOUTER'S NEW SCHOOL REGISTERS of the Study and Conduct of Young LADIES or GENTLEMEN, may be had on the shortest Notice, adapted for any School, with the Name and Address of the Establishment printed on the Cover.—From Copper-plates, Half Octavo Size, 9d. each, or 7s. per dozen. Neatly printed in Octavo, 1s. each, or 9s. per dozen. And beautifully printed in Script, on Super-fine Post Quarto, 2s. each, or 18s. per dozen.

N.B. *These Registers are adapted to any School, as they do not confine the Party to any particular Class of Books.*

SOUTER'S SCHOOL RECORDER; consisting of *Blank* Forms to be filled up agreeably to the particular Course of Study of each Pupil.— Octavo, price 1s. each, or 9s. per dozen.

HALF-YEARLY SCHOOL PRIZES;

OR

CHRISTMAS AND MIDSUMMER PRESENTS.

Proprietors of Schools, Private Teachers, and Parents, about to select their half-yearly Prizes, Christmas Presents, or New-Year's Gifts, are invited to inspect the EXTENSIVE COLLECTION of Books selected for that purpose, and constantly kept for sale, in a great variety of bindings, by J. SOUTER, at the

SCHOOL LIBRARY, 131, FLEET-STREET.

*** The Proprietors of Schools and Private Teachers are respectfully informed, that J. SOUTER's SCHOOL-MASTER's GENERAL CATALOGUE of upwards of 5000 SCHOOL-BOOKS in the various Languages, and in every Branch of Education, with their Prices annexed, may be had, as above.

*** BARDIN'S and CARY's GLOBES, all sizes, sold by J. SOUTER, on the same Terms as at the Maker's.

MATHEMATICAL and DRAWING INSTRUMENTS, of the best quality, supplied as cheap as at any House in London.

STAMPED SCHOOL MEDALS, a great variety, in White Metal, Copper, and Silver; from Sixpence to Fifteen Shillings each. Made also to Order.

N.B. PROPRIETORS of SCHOOLS may hear of ASSISTANTS, and TEACHERS of SITUATIONS, *without fee*, by applying to J. Souter, at the School Library, 131, Fleet Street.

PENKNIVES of superior quality, and lowest price.

A CATALOGUE

OF

ENGLISH, FRENCH, ITALIAN, GERMAN, LATIN, AND GREEK

BOOKS.

FIRST BOOKS.

1. THE ENGLISH PRIMER; or, Child's First Book: arranged on such a plan as cannot fail to delight young Children, and facilitate their instruction in the elements of Spelling and Reading. By the Rev. T. Clark. Illustrated by upwards of Two Hundred Wood-Engravings. 6d. sewed, or 10d. bound.

"This little Primer, at the moderate price of 6d. appears to justify what it promises in the title, being, of its kind, the most complete which has come under our notice."—*Gentleman's Magazine;* see also *Monthly Review,* &c.

2. The SAME in FRENCH. 1s. sewed, or 1s. 6d. bound.

3. THE ENGLISH MOTHER'S FIRST CATECHISM for her Children, containing those things most necessary to be known at an early age. Illustrated by One Hundred Engravings: being a Sequel to the above. By the Rev. T. Clark. 9d., or 1s. bound.

4. The SAME in FRENCH. 1s. sewed, or 1s. 6d. bound.

5. SOUTER'S PROGRESSIVE PRIMER, a First Book for Children, comprising both Spelling and Reading Lessons; arranged on a pleasing and simple principle, ascending by easy steps, calculated to interest and facilitate the progress of Children in an extraordinary degree. Leather backs. Price 6d.

6. INFANTINE STORIES, in Works of One, Two, and Three Syllables. New Edition. By Mrs. Fenwick. With six new Plates. 2s. half-bound.

"This is one of the most interesting books that can possibly be put into the hands of a Child, after Clark's excellent little Primer."

A 2

SPELLING-BOOKS AND DICTIONARIES.

1. SOUTER'S FIRST SCHOOL SPELLING-BOOK, on a simple and progressive principle; containing nearly every English Word in common use, arranged on an entirely new plan, calculated to facilitate the progress of Children in an uncommon degree. Each Table of Spelling is followed by an Easy Reading Lesson, containing only such Words as are to be found in the preceding Spelling Column: the whole forming a useful Introduction to the English Language. 1s. 6d. bd.

2. THE NATIONAL SPELLING-BOOK; or, Sure Guide to English Spelling and Pronunciation, on a plan which cannot fail to remove the difficulties, and facilitate general improvement, in the English Language. Revised by the Rev. T. Clark. 1s. 6d. bd.

3. THE ENGLISH SPELLING-BOOK and EXPO-SITOR: a New Edition, revised by the Rev. Thos. Smith, 12mo. 1s. 6d.

4. PIKE'S SPELLING, 12mo. bd. 1s. 6d.

5. ROBINSON'S SPELLING, 12mo. bd. 1s. 6d.

6. VYSE'S SPELLING, 12mo. bd. 1s. 6d.

7. BLAIR'S SCHOOL DICTIONARY, 12mo. bd. 3s.

8. ENTICK'S SPELLING DICTIONARY, improved by T. Browne, LL.D. Square. 2s. 6d. bd.

9. SHERIDAN IMPROVED; a General Pronouncing and Explanatory Dictionary of the English Language, for the use of Schools. Square. By S. Jones. 3s. 6d. bd.

10. A DICTIONARY of ENGLISH SYNONYMES: comprehending the Derivations and Meanings of the Words; and the Distinctions between the Synonymes, illustrated by Examples. By the Rev. John Platts. 5s. bds.

The writer felt the want of such a work as this during the many years he was engaged in the instruction of youth; and he has some confidence that this Dictionary will be favorably received by the respectable conductors of seminaries, and that it will be the means of assisting the English student in acquiring a knowledge of his native language, and the proper distinctions of words.

The Alphabetical Index at the end will at once exhibit all the words contained in the work, and direct to the page where each particular word may be found.

11. WORCESTER'S ENGLISH DICTIONARY, royal 12mo. 7s. 6d. bd.

12. CLASSICAL DICTIONARY. By Thos. Browne, LL.D. 12mo. 8s. bound.

MISCELLANEOUS READING.

1. SOUTER'S FIRST SCHOOL READER; comprising a Selection of Pleasing and Instructive Reading Lessons, progressively arranged, by means of which the Scholar is led, by gradual and regular steps, to the reading of English. The Lessons are suited to the capacity of youth, and treat of subjects calculated to interest as well as to inform. 2s. 6d. bound.

2. THE NATIONAL READER; consisting of Easy Lessons in Morals, History, Biography, Mythology, Natural History, Science, and General Knowledge; intended as a Sequel to the National Spelling-Book. By the Rev. T. Clark. Illustrated by numerous Engravings. A New Edition, improved and considerably enlarged, by Edward Wickes. 12mo. 3s. 6d. bd.

3. SOUTER'S SECOND SCHOOL READER; a Geographical Class-Book, containing concise Accounts of the Discoveries of the most celebrated Travellers; with Biographical Sketches. By G. A. Hansard. With Plates. 12mo. 4s. 6d. bd.

4. THE ELEMENTS OF READING; being Select and Easy Lessons in Prose and Verse, for young Readers of both Sexes. By the Rev. J. Adams, A.M. 3s. 6d. bound.

5. THE DICTATE BOOK; being Lessons on Life, Men, and Manners. By the Rev. George Hall, M.A. Vicar of Tenbury, Worcestershire; Rector of Rochford, Herefordshire; and Chaplain to Lord Brougham and Vaux. 4s. neatly bound.

Here the path to Riches, Reputation, and Happiness is marked out, and directions for forming the Mind, the Morals, and Manners, set forth.

6. SELECT PLAYS FROM SHAKSPEARE, adapted chiefly for the use of Schools and Young Persons, with Notes, from the best Commentators. By Edward Slater, Queen's College, Cambridge.

This selection comprises the following admired Plays, viz. HAMLET, MACBETH, RICHARD III., KING JOHN, CORIOLANUS, and JULIUS CÆSAR.

This elegant Volume is strongly recommended to the Heads of Families and Schools, as comprising the most admired Plays of the illustrious Author, with the omission of all objectionable matter. At the same time it is to be observed, that very little variation from the Original will be recognized in these pages, as the Editor has sought to give Shakspeare in all his INTEGRITY, with the single deduction necessary to render him available for Youth. He has thus preserved, with the slightest infringement, the interest justly attached to the reading of an original work, conscious that any departure from this rule, not sanctioned by the highest reasons, would obtain no favour from the present age. Guided by this principle, he trusts he may claim to have produced a Shakspeare that will meet the views of the judicious Instructors of Youth of both sexes, and supply the means long sought, he conceives—of bringing this first of Authors, and glory of his country, under the notice of their youthful charge.

Price 7s. 6d. neatly done up in cloth; or each Play separate, 1s. 6d. cloth.

7. BIBLE LETTERS for CHILDREN, by Lucy Barton ;
with Introductory Verses by Bernard Barton, new edition, fine, with
frontispiece, 3s. half-bound. Cheap edition, for Sunday Schools. 2s.

"We think this little volume does infinite credit to the youthful writer. The
selections are very judicious ; and the lessons dwelt upon and explained in a simple
manner, obvious to the most juvenile capacity."—*Literary Gazette*, August 27, 1831.

" This is one of the best books for young persons that we have seen for a long
time. The style is very easy and natural, and the whole work. excellent."—*Home
Missionary*, September 1, 1831.

" Although we do not often notice books of this class, we have great pleasure in
recommending this as one that will become a favorite."—*New Monthly Magazine*,
Oct. 1, 1831.

" We almost envy the parent whose young daughter has talent and grace sufficient
to enable her to write such letters as these for the rising generation."—*Evangelical
Magazine*, Oct. 1, 1831.

" Parents will find this volume well suited for interesting and instructing the
juvenile branches of their families."—*World*, August 22, 1831.

8. MORNINGS IN THE LIBRARY, by Ann Knight.
With Introductory Lines and Concluding Poem, by Bernard Barton.
18mo. 2s. 6d. half-bound.

9. DIURNAL READINGS, 12mo. 5s. 6d. bound.

10. GAY'S FABLES, 18mo. 2s. 6d. half-bound.

11. THE FABLES of ÆSOP. By S. Croxall. 3s. 6d. bd.
A fine Edition of the above, with One Hundred and Eleven Plates.
12mo. 12s. bds.

12. THE LOOKING-GLASS for the MIND; or Intellectual Mirror. With Seventy-four Cuts. 3s. 6d. bd.

13. THE BLOSSOMS of MORALITY; intended for the
Amusement and Instruction of Young Gentlemen. By the editor of
" The Looking-glass for the Mind." With Forty-seven Cuts, by
Bewick. 18mo. 2s. 6d. half-bound.

14. A TOUR of ASIA, compiled from the best Works of
Modern Travellers ; illustrated with Maps and Engravings. By the
Rev. T. Clark. 5s. bd.

15. THE TRAVELS of POLYCLETES: a Series of Let-
ters on the Manners, Customs, Laws, Institutions, and General History of the Romans. By M. le Baron de Théis, abridged by M. de
Rouillon, and translated by M. A. P. 12mo. 6s. 6d. boards.

16. The SAME may be had in FRENCH. 6s. 6d.

" The volume before us will doubtless prove an important assistant to young
beginners in the study of ancient history : by all classes it will be read with pleasure
and utility, as containing much information concerning the public and private life
of the Romans, their laws both civil and military, their literature, their arts and
sciences, and, in short, their manners and customs in each particular."—*Monthly
Magazine*.

———

SOUTER'S IMPROVED SERIES

OF

DR. IRVING'S CATECHISMS.

New Editions, revised by Dr. Busby; the Rev. T. Clark; J. G. Gorton; C. Mackenzie; Wm. Maugham; F. W. Simms; J. T. Pratt, Esq., &c. 9d. sewed, or 1s. strongly bound.

*** To render these Catechisms every way deserving the very extensive patronage they have received, no expense will be spared in the revision and improvement of each and every edition;—many of the present editions are nearly double the size of the former, without any advance of price, and they have from time to time been revised and improved by men of the first eminence in Science and Literature.

The proprietor can now, without fear of competition, offer them to the public as the best and cheapest publications of the day.

1. HISTORY of ENGLAND; containing the most striking events from the earliest Period to the present Time. By C. Irving, LL.D. F.A.S.; a new edition revised and improved, to which are added Chronological Tables of the Kings of England, and the contemporary Sovereigns; illustrated by a beautiful Engraving of Cardinal Langton and the Barons at St. Edmond's Bury.

2. GEOGRAPHY of ENGLAND and WALES; containing an accurate description of their Situation, Extent, Divisions, Population, Soil, Climate, Mountains, Rivers, Lakes, Canals, Islands, and Capes, with a compendious account of the chief Towns, Commerce, Manufactures; Vegetable, Animal, and Mineral productions of each county. By C. Irving, LL.D., F.A.S., new edition with a Map.

3. HISTORY of IRELAND; containing the most striking events of that country, from the earliest Period of authentic history to the present Time. By J. G. Gorton. Embellished with Portraits.

4. GEOGRAPHY of IRELAND; containing an accurate description of its Situation, Extent, Provinces, Counties, Parishes, Baronies, Mountains, Rivers, Canals, Lakes, and the chief Towns, Manufactures, &c. By C. Irving, LL.D., F.A.S., with a Map.

5. HISTORY of SCOTLAND; containing a concise account of every striking event in that country from the earliest Period of authentic history to the present Time. By C. Irving, LL.D. F.A.S., Embellished with Portraits.

6. GEOGRAPHY of SCOTLAND; containing an accurate description of its Situation, Extent, Districts, Parishes, Population, Rivers, Lakes, Canals, Islands, and Capes; the chief Towns, Commerce, Manufactures, &c. By C. Irving, LL.D. F.A.S., with a Map.

7. HISTORY of FRANCE; containing a concise account of the most striking events of that country, from the earliest Period to the present Time. By J. G. Gorton, with Portraits.

8. GEOGRAPHY of FRANCE; containing a description of its Situation, Extent, Departments, Population, Soil, Climate, Mountains, Rivers, &c.; with an account of the chief Towns, Commerce, Manufactures; Vegetable, Animal, and Mineral productions of each department. By C. Irving, LL.D. F.A.S., with a Map.

9. HISTORY of GREECE, from the earliest Times to the Period when Greece became a Roman province. By C. Irving, LL.D. F.A.S. with Portraits.

10. ANTIQUITIES of GREECE; being an account of the Religion, Government, Judicial Proceedings, Military and Naval Affairs, Coins, Weights, Measures, &c. By C. Irving, LL.D.

11. HISTORY of ROME; containing a concise account of the most striking events from the Foundation of the city to the Fall of the Western empire. By C. Irving, LL.D. F.A.S.

12. ANTIQUITIES of ROME; being an account of the Religion, Civil Government, Military, and Naval Affairs, Games, Coins, Weights, and Measures, Dress, Food, Exercises, Baths, Domestic Employments, Marriages, Funerals, and other Customs and Ceremonies. By C. Irving, LL.D. F.A.S.

13. SACRED HISTORY; as related in the Old and New Testaments, &c.; for the use of Schools. By C. Irving, LL.D. F.A.S., new edition revised by the Rev. T. Clark, and illustrated with a Map of Palestine.

14. UNIVERSAL HISTORY; containing a concise account of the most striking events from the earliest Period to the present Time. By C. Irving, LL.D. New edition by J. G. Gorton.

15. GENERAL GEOGRAPHY; being an e introduction to a Knowledge of the Situation and Extent of every country in the world; with an account of the Mountains, Lakes, Rivers, Religion, Government, &c. By C. Irving, LL.D.; with Maps.

16. JEWISH ANTIQUITIES; containing an account of the Classes, Institutions, Rites, Ceremonies, Manners, Customs, &c. of the Ancient Jews. By C. Irving, LL.D. F.A.S., with Plates.

17. CLASSICAL BIOGRAPHY; containing an account of the Lives of the most celebrated Characters among the Ancient Greeks and Romans. By C. Irving, LL.D. F.A.S., with Portraits.

18. CATECHISM of ASTRONOMY; containing the Motions, Magnitude, Periods, Distances, and other Phenomena of the Heavenly Bodies, founded on the Laws of Gravitation: illustrated by plates. By C. Irving, LL.D. F.A.S. New Edition by F. W. Simms, assistant Astronomer at the Royal Observatory, Greenwich,

19. BOTANY; containing a description of some of the most Familiar and Interesting Plants; arranged according to the Linnæan System; with an Appendix on the Formation of an Herbarium. By C. Irving, LL.D. 9d. plain, or 1s. with the plates colored.

20. THE BRITISH CONSTITUTION; containing a view of the Privileges, Rights, and Liberties of King and People; the Constitution and Functions of both Houses of Parliament; and the Duties of the Great Officers of State, Ministers of the Crown, and the Magistracy generally. With an Analysis of the several Orders of Society, the Courts of Justice, and other Political Institutions of the British Empire. By John Tidd Pratt, Esq. barrister-at-law.

21. ENGLISH GRAMMAR; carefully compiled from the best authors, with numerous Exercises. By C. Irving, LL.D. F.A.S.; new edition revised and considerably enlarged by E. Wickes.

22. FRENCH GRAMMAR; carefully compiled from the best authors; chiefly intended as an introduction to MM. Hamel's, Levizac's, and Rouillon's Grammars. By A. Gombert, Professor of the French Language; and editor of Moliere's, Racine's, and Corneille's Plays, with Notes Critical and Explanatory; new edition, with Exercises on the Rules, by J. C. Tarver, French Professor, Eton College.

23. ITALIAN GRAMMAR; carefully compiled from the best authors; intended as an introduction to the Study of the Italian Language. By A. Gombert, Professor of Languages.

24. GENERAL KNOWLEDGE; containing much useful information in the Arts and Sciences, and Literature, necessary to be known at an early Age. By C. Irving, LL.D. F.A.S., with Plates.

25. CATECHISM of CHEMISTRY; exhibiting a concise view of the present state of the Science; illustrated by plates. By W. Maugham, Lecturer on Chemistry at the Gallery of Practical Science, Adelaide street, and at the Charing-cross Hospital.

26. MUSIC; in which the Elementary Principles of the Science are fully and clearly explained; with preliminary instructions for the Piano-forte. By T. Busby, Mus. Doc.

27. MYTHOLOGY; being a compendious History of the Heathen Gods, Goddesses, and Heroes; designed chiefly as an introduction to the Study of the Classics. By C. Irving, LL.D., with Plates.

28. NATURAL PHILOSOPHY. By C. Mackenzie, author of Experiments in Chemistry, &c.

₀ These may be had in 4 vols. half-bound, price 24s.

THE ENGLISH MOTHER'S CATECHISM for her Children; containing those Things most necessary to be known at an early Age; illustrated by 100 Engravings. By the Rev. T. Clark. 9d. sd.

IMPROVED SERIES

OF

W. G. LEWIS'S CATECHISMS

OF

THE ARTS AND SCIENCES.

PRICE SIXPENCE EACH.

Elementary books like the following, must of necessity be, in a great measure, mere compilations, and the principal portion of originality to which the Editor can lay claim, consists in his plan, and in the introduction of Etymological and Pronouncing Vocabularies of the technical terms.

The great advantages resulting from the introduction of the Technical Vocabularies, are too obvious to require any observation. The Editor, however, may be allowed to remark, that technical terms being for the most part derived from the learned languages, the reason of their application is completely unseen by the mere English student; and the consequence is, that he finds them exceedingly difficult to remember. The Greek characters are, therefore, represented by English letters.

In these Catechisms the questions do not precede the answers, as in the series by Dr. Irving, &c., but are printed at the end of each part. To avoid, however, any difficulty, each question is numbered so as to answer to its corresponding proposition, which is also numbered. By this plan the tutor may either teach by interrogation or not; and persons, who may use the work for their own instruction, or for the purpose of reference, will not be confused and interrupted by a number of superfluous questions.

As school-books, they will be found to possess many advantages over the common catechisms; not the least of which is their capability of being used as reading-books for classes; in which case, if the tutor employ the questions in interrogating his pupils, they will be found peculiarly useful to exercising the memory, as well as in enforcing attention to the subject.

·1. ARCHITECTURE; Civil, and Military, on a new plan, illustrated by engravings; to which is added an Etymological and Pronouncing Vocabulary of the Technical Terms.

2. ASTRONOMY; on a new plan, illustrated by engravings; to which is added an Etymological and Pronouncing Vocabulary of the Technical Terms.

3. MECHANICS; on a new plan, illustrated by Twenty-eight engravings; to which is added an Etymological and Pronouncing Vocabulary of the Technical Terms.

·4. NATURAL HISTORY of MAN; illustrated by Engravings, to which is added an Etymological and Pronouncing Vocabulary of Technical Terms.

5. NATURAL HISTORY of BEASTS; Part I.; on a new plan, illustrated by engravings; to which is added an Etymological and Pronouncing Vocabulary of the Technical Terms.

6. NATURAL HISTORY of BEASTS; Part II.; on a new plan, illustrated by engravings; to which is added an Etymological and Pronouncing Vocabulary of the Technical Terms.

7. NATURAL HISTORY of BIRDS; Part I.; on a new plan, illustrated by engravings; to which is added an Etymological and Pronouncing Vocabulary of the Technical Terms.

8. NATURAL HISTORY of BIRDS; Part II.; on a new plan, illustrated by engravings; to which is added an Etymological and Pronouncing Vocabulary of the Technical Terms.

9. NATURAL HISTORY of AMPHIBIOUS ANIMALS; on a new plan, illustrated by engravings; to which is added an Etymological and Pronouncing Vocabulary of the Technical Terms.

10. NATURAL HISTORY of FISHES; on a new plan, illustrated by engravings; to which is added an Etymological and Pronouncing Vocabulary of the Technical Terms.

11. NATURAL HISTORY of INSECTS; with an Appendix, containing the Natural History of Worms; on a new plan, illustrated by engravings; to which is added an Etymological and Pronouncing Vocabulary of the Technical Terms.

12. HYDROSTATICS; on a new plan, illustrated by engravings; to which is added an Etymological and Pronouncing Vocabulary of the Technical Terms.

13. PNEUMATICS; on a new plan, illustrated by engravings; to which is added an Etymological and Pronouncing Vocabulary of the Technical Terms.

14. HYDRAULICS; on a new plan, illustrated by engravings; to which is added an Etymological and Pronouncing Vocabulary of the Technical Terms.

15. OPTICS; on a new plan, illustrated by engravings; to which is added an Etymological and Pronouncing Vocabulary of the Technical Terms.

16. ACOUSTICS; on a new plan, illustrated by engravings; to which is added an Etymological and Pronouncing Vocabulary of the Technical Terms.

17. MAGNETISM; on a new plan, illustrated by engravings; to which is added an Etymological and Pronouncing Vocabulary of the Technical Terms.

18. ELECTRICITY; on a new plan, illustrated by engravings; to which is added an Etymological and Pronouncing Vocabulary of the Technical Terms.

⁎ These may be had in 2 vols. bound, 9s. or the vol. on Natural History, 4s. 6d. and the volume on the Arts and Sciences, 5s.

COMPOSITION, ELOCUTION, &c.

1. THE RHETORICAL SPEAKER and POETICAL CLASS-BOOK; comprising Prefatory Observations on the Origin and Structure of Language; an Analysis of Poetry, in which the various tropes and figures are illustrated by the most striking and beautiful extracts; Directions for the proper modulation of the Voice, the delineation of the Passions, &c., together with a new and choice Selection of Pieces, from the most esteemed authors, adapted to Recitation and Reading, with copious instructions for their appropriate delivery. By R. T. Linnington, Teacher of Elocution, &c. 4s. neatly bound.

*** The Rhetorical Speaker will be found to contain a collection of the finest poetry in the language, and the most suitable for Recitation and Reading. Several of the pieces are original, and very few of them have ever appeared in similar works. It also embodies much interesting and useful information on Language in general, and on the English Language in particular. The character of Poetry, and the laws of Versification, are treated in a comprehensive and perspicuous manner; and the figures of Rhetoric are exemplified by the finest poetical gems.

2. THE SCIENTIFIC READER. By R. T. Linnington. 12mo. 3s. bound.

3. ENFIELD'S SCHOOL SPEAKER. 12mo. 3s. 6d. bd.

4. A DICTIONARY of ENGLISH SYNONYMES: comprehending the Derivations and Meanings of the Words; and the Distinctions between the Synonymes, illustrated by Examples. By the Rev. John Platts. 5s.

5. ORTHOGRAPHICAL EXERCISES, in a Series of Moral Letters: to which is added, a Selection of Essays, &c. taken from the best English Writers. By the late James Alderson. New Edition, revised by the Rev. Thomas Smith. 18mo. 1s. bound.

6. WALKER'S ACADEMIC SPEAKER. New Edition. 12mo. 4s. bound.

7. WALKER'S THEMES and ESSAYS. 12mo. 4s. bd.

8. A SYSTEM of RHETORIC for the use of Schools. By J. Stirling, D.D. 12mo. 6d. sewed.

GEOGRAPHY, HISTORY, THE USE OF THE GLOBES, AND ASTRONOMY.

1. THE GEOGRAPHICAL TEXT-BOOK; a practical Geography, calculated to facilitate the study of that useful Science, by a constant reference to the Blank Maps; according to the plan pursued in Pestalozzian and other Establishments. By M. E°°° S°°°°°. Part I. Comprising the General Geography of the Six Grand Divisions of the Earth: Europe, Africa, Asia, Australasia, Polynesia, and America; with the Etymology and Pronunciation given throughout. Price 2s. cloth.

"The Geographical Text-Book, as its name implies, consists only of such matter as is necessary to be impressed deeply and lastingly upon the memory of the student. The First Part comprehends those general principles reduced to their simplest form, which are the groundwork of the whole science."

Extract from the London Magazine and Journal of Educational Institutions, Oct. 1836.—"Considering the value of the science of geography, it is of the greatest importance that, in instructing youth in its elements, the means of imparting that instruction should be made as simple as possible. There is such a want of proper arrangement and simplification in the geographical school books in general, that we are persuaded much time, which might be employed advantageously by the pupil and by the teacher, is completely wasted. All that is necessary to be done, is to convey to the understanding of the pupils a thorough knowledge of the simple elements of the science; and when they have acquired that, to carry them on gradually to the minutiæ of the subject. 'For too much care,' says the writer, 'cannot be taken to bring the pupils *gradually* on, and to feel convinced that they understand perfectly one paragraph before proceeding to the next.' Instead of this plan being adopted in the works generally used at scholastic establishments, the whole is jumbled together, without selection and without proper arrangement, into one small book; and the result is, that the pupil is confused and bewildered.

"The little book before us is, we think, admirably adapted to obviate this difficulty. It is written clearly and concisely, and the different heads are judiciously arranged. It is peculiarly adapted for schools, both public and private; but, perhaps, the best we can say of it is, that it is written upon the system of *Pestalozzi*. The scientific information is given in the first portion of the book, and the latter part consists of questions relating to the former. The questions for examination are well arranged; and in all we see the *why* and the *wherefore* put into operation. This plan cannot fail to impress the subjects thoroughly on the minds of the pupils; we, therefore, recommend the Geographical Text Book to instructors of youth, and to institutions for the improvement of the people, as being one well worthy of their consideration. The maps which accompany this work are beautifully executed, and will greatly facilitate the study of the science."

2. THE BLANK MAPS done up separately, price 2s. plain, or 2s. 6d. colored.

"This volume of Blank Maps will form an invaluable companion to any elementary work on Geography, published without such an useful Auxiliary, and may therefore be had separately."

3. The TEXT-BOOK of ANCIENT GEOGRAPHY, in the Press.

4. OUTLINES of GEOGRAPHY, for the use of Children, by the Misses Owen. 12mo. 1s. sewed.

5. CLARK'S MODERN GEOGRAPHY and HISTORY, containing an Account of the present State of the Kingdoms of the World, with the political Alterations determined by the Congress of Vienna: to which is annexed, a Series of Questions for the exercise and examination of the Student. A new Edition, improved. 4s. 6d.

6. GEOGRAPHY and HISTORY; by a Lady. 4s. 6d. bd.

7. GEOGRAPHY on a new Plan; by T. Keith. 6s. bd.

8. An ABRIDGMENT of ANCIENT GEOGRAPHY, in short Lessons, intended as a Sequel to the above. By the Abbé du Fresnoy. 2s. 6d. cloth.

9. ADAMS'S GEOGRAPHY and HISTORY. 8vo. 15s. bd.

10. GUTHRIE'S GEOGRAPHY; large 8vo. 18s. boards.

11. GUTHRIE'S ATLAS. 8vo. 10s. 6d. colored.

12. BROOKES'S GAZETTEER. 8vo. 12s. boards.

13. CATECHISM of the GEOGRAPHY of ENGLAND and WALES.—13. of IRELAND.—14. of SCOTLAND.—15. of FRANCE.—16. And of GENERAL GEOGRAPHY. By C. Irving, LL.D. F.S.A. 9d. each, or 1s. bound.

14. GEOGRAPHY for CHILDREN; by Mme. du Fresnoy. 12mo. 2s. bound.

15. A NEW SCHOOL ATLAS of ANCIENT and MODERN GEOGRAPHY: exhibiting the various Divisions of the World, with the chief Empires, Kingdoms, and States; in Forty-three Maps, carefully corrected from the latest and best Authorities. Royal 4to. colored; with an Index containing the ancient and modern Names, with the Latitudes and Longitudes of every place as given in the Maps. By the Rev. T. Clark. 21s.

16. THE ATLAS of MODERN GEOGRAPHY, separately. Royal 8vo. colored, with an Index. 12s.

17. THE ATLAS of ANCIENT GEOGRAPHY, separately. With an Index of ancient and modern Names. 10s. 6d.

18. THE MINOR ATLAS; containing Twelve of the most useful Maps for Beginners, viz. The World, Europe, England and Wales, Scotland, Ireland, France, Spain and Portugal, Asia, Hindoostan, Africa, North America and South America. New Edition. Half-bound, 5s. colored.

" For clearness, accuracy, and cheapness, these Atlases are unequalled by any now extant."

19. THE MINOR GEOGRAPHICAL COPY-BOOKS,
adapted to the Minor Atlas, No. 1, containing Twelve corresponding
Outlines, to be filled up by the younger Pupils. Oblong 4to. sewed,
2s. 6d., and 3s. 6d. colored.

20. Ditto, No. 2, containing Twelve Projections of Maps,
or Lines of Latitude and Longitude only. 2s. 6d.

₀ With the assistance of these Copy-Books a student will acquire a more perfect
knowledge of Geography in a few months, than in as many years without such aid.

21. CLARK'S NEW SERIES of SCHOOL MAPS,
Ancient and Modern, from the latest and best Authorities; sold separately, 6d. each, colored:
Comprising, 1. The World. 2. Mercator's Projection of the World.
3. Europe. 4. England. 5. Scotland. 6. Ireland. 7. France in Provinces. 8. France in Departments. 9. Russia. 10. Spain and Portugal.
11. Turkey and Hungary. 12. Poland. 13. Holland and the Nether-
lands. 14. Sweden and Norway. 15. Denmark. 16. Germany. 17. Swit-
zerland. 18. Italy. 19. Asia. 20. Modern Persia. 21. China. 22. Hindoostan. 23. East Indies. 24. Africa. 25. North America. 26. West
Indies. 27. South America. 28. Canaan, or Judea. 29. Travels of St.
Paul. 30. Græcia Antiqua. 31. Italia Antiqua. 32. Imperium Per-
sicum Antiquum. 33. Romanum Imperium. 34. Gallia Antiqua. 35.
Britannia Antiqua. 36. Expeditio Hannibalis. 37. Syria and Assyria.
38. Asia Minor. 39. Germania Antiqua. 40. Terra Veteribus Nota.
41. Hispania Antiqua. 42. Africa Antiqua. 43. Ægyptus Antiqua.

22. FORTY-THREE NEW OUTLINE MAPS, on the
same Scale as the above, and in which the chief Cities, Towns, Rivers,
Lakes, and Mountains are all laid down, but their Names omitted, to
be filled up by junior Pupils. 4d. each, or 6d. colored.

23. FORTY-THREE PROJECTIONS, on the same
Scale as the above, to be filled up by senior Pupils. 4d. each.

24. AN ALPHABETICAL INDEX, with the Ancient
and Modern Names, Longitudes, and Latitudes, of all Places mentioned in these Maps, may be had to the Twenty-seven Modern Maps;
price 2s. 6d.; to the Ancient Maps, 1s. 6d.; or to the whole complete, 3s. 6d.

25. BELOE'S OUTLINE MAPS. 1. WESTERN
HEMISPHERE. 2. EASTERN HEMISPHERE. 3. EUROPE.
4. ENGLAND and WALES. 5. ASIA. 6. AFRICA. 7. NORTH
AMERICA. 8. SOUTH AMERICA. Each 15 Inches by 14. Price 1s.
on superfine drawing paper, or 1s. 6d. on Bristol boards.

1. ANCIENT HISTORY; exhibiting a summary View of the Rise, Progress, Revolutions, Decline, and Fall of the States and Nations of Antiquity. By John Robinson, D.D. Rector of Clifton, Westmoreland, and author of the "Grammar of History," "Antiquities of Greece," &c. A new Edition, enlarged and improved; with a Series of Questions on the most important Points of History, and illustrated by Five coloured Maps. 9s. 6d. neatly bound in green and lettered.

"We may safely recommend this work as one of the most useful of its class."—Literary Gazette, Nov. 26, 1831.

2. THE HISTORY of ENGLAND, with the Contemporary Sovereigns and distinguished Characters of each Reign, from the Reformation to the present time. By Miss C. A. Davies. With Portraits of their Majesties and his Grace the Duke of Wellington. 5s.

3. FLORIAN'S GUIDE to the STUDY of the HISTORY of ENGLAND. By J. G. Gorton. 1s. 6d. bd.

4. FLORIAN'S GUIDE to the HISTORY of ROME. 1s.

5. GOLDSMITH'S ABRIDGMENT of the HISTORY of ENGLAND; with upwards of One Thousand Questions for Exercise. Brought down to the present time. By J. Dymock. 12mo. 4s. bd.

6. GOLDSMITH'S ABRIDGMENT of the HISTORY of ROME. 12mo., with a colored Map of Ancient Rome. 3s. 6d. bd.

7. FIVE HUNDRED QUESTIONS deduced from the Abridgment of Goldsmith's History of Rome: to which are prefixed, a brief Sketch of the Roman Polity, and of the principal constituted authorities of the Romans, in the most flourishing times of the Commonwealth; a Table of the Roman Emperors, of the most celebrated Roman Authors, and their Works. By J. G. Gorton. 1s. sewed.

8. GOLDSMITH'S ABRIDGMENT of the HISTORY of GREECE. 12mo., with a colored Map of Ancient Greece. 3s. 6d.

9. FIVE HUNDRED QUESTIONS deduced from Goldsmith's History of Greece, on the plan of the above. By the same Author. 1s. sewed.

10. A KEY to the Questions on Goldsmith's Histories of Greece and Rome; by the same Author. 1s. sewed.

11. ADAMS'S HISTORY of GREAT BRITAIN. 4s. 6d.

12. ADAMS'S HISTORY of ROME. 4s. 6d. bd.

13. BIGLAND'S LETTERS on ANCIENT & MODERN HISTORY. 6s. bd.

14. A CONCISE INTRODUCTION to the KNOWLEDGE of the GLOBES. By Thomas Molineux. 3s. bound.

15. BONNYCASTLE'S ASTRONOMY. 8vo. 12s. bds.

———

5

WRITING, ARITHMETIC, AND BOOK-KEEPING.

WRITING.

1. AN ANALYSIS of PENMANSHIP; containing Rules and Observations on the Formation of each Letter; together with a Projection of the Alphabet, and Specimens of Writing. By J. Hill. 5s.

2. HILL'S GEOGRAPHICAL COPY SLIPS, viz. Large-hand; Text-hand; Round-hand; and Small-hand. Price 6d. each.

3. HILL'S NEW SLIP COPIES, Nos. 1 and 2 (Small-hand;) comprising a Course of elegant Extracts from Addison and others, each subject occupying about half a page in the Copy-book, so as to prevent the pupil copying his own writing. 6d. each.

4. SOUTER'S HISTORICAL SLIPS. Small-hand. 6d.

5. ————— SMALL - HAND SLIPS; comprising Passages from Shakspeare, Addison, Cowper, Thomson, and Gay. 6d.

6. ————— SMALL-HAND SLIPS; comprising Bills of Exchange, Promissory Notes, and Receipts. 6d.

7. ————— RUNNING-HAND COPIES, for Ladies, in French; comprising Recueil de Billets, choisies à l'Usage des jeunes Demoiselles. 6d.

8. ————— ROUND-HAND COPIES; comprising Clark's Latin Apophthegms; consisting of Lines from Cicero, Terence, Horace, Virgil, Seneca, Tacitus, Florus, Ovid, and Persius. 6d.

9. ————— SMALL-HAND COPIES; comprising Latin Examples of Syntax. 6d.

ARITHMETIC.

1. THE FIRST FOUR RULES of ARITHMETIC, on a Plan entirely original, calculated to abridge the labor of the Tutor very considerably, and to greatly facilitate the progress of the Pupil. By J. Walker. 1s. 6d. bound.

AN EXPOSITION of the SYSTEM is printed, and sold at 2s., sealed up; which will only be delivered to Schoolmasters or Teachers who apply personally, or by letter addressed to the publisher.

2. WALKER'S NEW CIPHERING-BOOK, on the same System; Part I. containing the Simple Rules: neatly printed in Script, on fine foolscap 4to. 3s. half-bound.

3. WALKER'S NEW CIPHERING-BOOK, Part II. containing the Compound Rules; printed uniformly with the above. 3s. neatly half-bound.

4. THE SECOND BOOK OF ARITHMETIC, for Pupils who have passed through the First Four Rules. By Wm. Russell, author of "Philosophy of Arithmetic." 2s. bound.

5. THE PHILOSOPHY OF ARITHMETIC; or a Complete Analysis of Integers, for the use of advanced Students, but suited to the most limited capacity: also an Appendix, containing Domestic Calculations, to be performed mentally. By Wm. Russell, Writing-Master and Accomptant. 1s. 6d.

₊ This work " will be found useful in exciting an interest in the young mind as it regards the science. The pupil who is so unfortunate as to have a stiff unphilosophical tutor, who will not, or cannot, explain the principles of Arithmetic, will find this work a useful and valuable companion."—*Education Review*, July 1895.

6. A KEY TO RUSSELL'S SECOND BOOK; containing Solutions of all the Questions and Examples. By Wm. Russell, 2s. 6d. bd.

7. A NEW ARITHMETIC for YOUNG LADIES. By Mrs. E. English. 12mo. 1s. bound.

8. SOUTER'S NEW CIPHERING-BOOK for BEGINNERS; containing the first Four Rules of Arithmetic, Simple and Compound. By R. W. Part I. Beautifully printed on fine post 4to. after the manner of copper-plate. 1s. 6d.

9. A KEY to the ABOVE, giving eight Solutions of every Sum, correctly worked at length. 4s.

10. SOUTER'S NEW CIPHERING-BOOK. Part II., for more advanced Pupils. 3s. 6d. half-bound.

11. A KEY to the ABOVE, giving eight Answers to every Sum worked at length. 8s. half-bound.

So much pains has been taken with these books that the author can almost vouch for there not being a single error; and he engages to give certain premiums, mentioned in the Prefaces, to any pupil who may discover an error.

12. SOUTER'S COMPLETE SET of ARITHMETICAL TABLES, on a large 8vo. card, 4d., or 3s. 4d. per dozen; or, large 4to. 6d., or 5s. per dozen.

13. SOUTER'S MINOR TABLE CARDS; a smaller size than the above. 2d., or 1s. 8d. per dozen.

14. TAPLIN'S IMPROVED EDITION of WALKIN-GAME'S TUTOR'S ASSISTANT, for the Use of Schools: containing Rules for Working the various Methods of Calculation, with Questions under every respective Title: to which is added, An APPENDIX on CIRCULATING DECIMALS, By R. H. Nicholls. 2s. 6d. bound: or, with a Short System of Book-keeping, 6d. extra.

THE BOOK-KEEPING separately, 1s. sewed.

15. TAPLIN'S KEY to the ABOVE, with all the Answers worked at length. 12mo. price 9s.

16. BEASLEY'S ARITHMETICAL TABLE - BOOK, with the new Imperial Weights and Measures; containing also the French Weights and Measures, and a System of Mental Reckoning. 6d.

17. BONNYCASTLE'S ARITHMETIC. 8vo. 8s. boards.

18. —— ARITHMETIC. 12mo. 3s. 6d. bd.—KEY. 4s. 6d.

19. —— ALGEBRA. 2 vol. 8vo. £1.5s. bds.

20. —— ALGEBRA. 12mo. 4s.—KEY. 4s. 6d.

21. —— MENSURATION. 12mo. 4s. 6d.—KEY. 4s.

22. —— ASTRONOMY. 8vo. boards, 12s.

23. —— GEOMETRY. 8vo. boards, 10s. 6d.

24. KEITH'S ARITHMETIC. 4s. 6d.—KEY. 5s. 6d.

25. GOODACRE'S ARITHMETIC. 4s.—KEY. 6s.

BOOK-KEEPING.

1. THE SCHOLAR'S INTRODUCTION to MERCHANTS' ACCOUNTS: practically adapted to the use of schools; comprising the Waste Book, with instructive Notes under every transaction, wherein he is taught, by double entry, the Method of Journalising the Waste-Book, Posting the Journal, and Balancing the Ledger, without the necessity of having before him the Journal and Ledger for reference. The whole exemplified upon a newly arranged Principle, calculated to facilitate the improvement of the learner. By George Reynolds, Writing-Master, Christ's Hospital. Second Edition. 6s. 6d.

" Whatever tends to induce the learner to think or reason on a subject; whatever tends to excite in the mind a desire to study the object before him, must be of the greatest importance."

2. NUMERICAL KEY for the USE of the TEACHER. 1s.

3. TWO SETS of BLANK BOOKS, in 4to., prepared and ruled for the use of the Learner. Part I. 4s.; Part II. 5s.

" This is a very excellent treatise on Book-keeping, and is well worthy the attention of teachers as well as scholars. The rules and instructions given are at once perfectly simple, clear, and comprehensive; and it is therefore, as a school-book, admirably suited to every capacity. We feel every confidence in saying that it requires only to be better known in order to ensure its general use; and therefore the public at large are much indebted to Mr. Reynolds for presenting them with this opportunity of easily acquiring such a perfect knowledge of book-keeping as, if fully practised, will certainly go far to ensure success in their operations, and to exempt them from much misfortune."—*Edinburgh Literary Gazette.*

".Mr. Reynolds has here presented us with a new and very ingenious method of book-keeping, which is well deserving the notice of those to whom the task of instructing youth is intrusted. Mr. Reynolds's object has been to simplify the system, by reducing the number of books heretofore considered necessary to condense the labour, without interfering with the accuracy of the counting-house arrangements; and we think that he has succeeded in effecting that desirable object, and has thereby conferred a great benefit on the commercal part of the community."—*Brit. Traveller.*

" We have looked over this treatise upon merchants' accounts with much satisfaction. It is arranged upon a new and simple plan, by which the scholar, instead of being made to copy mechanically the journal and ledger, is placed under the necessity of actually studying the subject before him. We recommend the work to the attention both of teachers and men of business.'—*Edinburgh Literary Journal.*

" We warmly recommend Mr. Reynolds's Introduction to Merchants' Accounts, it exhibits important improvements."—*Gentleman's Magazine.*

" Mr. Reynolds, very much superior to most of his brethren, seems to have been perfectly conversant with the grand secret for preparing all elementary works; namely, to take for granted that the persons into whose hands the book was to fall knew nothing whatever of the matter treated of beforehand. The writer who does not proceed on such an assumption as this, can scarcely expect to add much in his day to the facilities for communicating instruction. It is in the very nature of productions of this sort to be incapable of being duly appreciated through the medium of general description or detached portions. We can only say, that it is well worthy the attention of heads of families and of schools; and, from what we learn of the state of some of our public offices, we think that Mr. Reynolds would be doing a patriotic act by sending a couple of copies to his Grace of Wellington, who has been declared by a public commission not long ago not to be a man of account."—*Monthly Review.*

4. KELLY'S (P., LL.D.) ELEMENTS of BOOK-KEEPING; comprising a System of Merchants' Accounts, founded on real Business: with an Appendix on Exchanges, Banking, and other Commercial Subjects. 8vo. 7s. bound.

5. KELLY'S BLANK BOOKS, adapted to the above. 5s.

6. ——————————— Third Set. 12s.

ANALYTICAL COURSE OF MATHEMATICS,

By J. R. Young, Professor of Mathematics, Royal College, Belfast.

1. ELEMENTS of GEOMETRY; containing a New and Universal Treatise on the Doctrine of Proportion, together with Notes, in which are pointed out and corrected several important Errors that have hitherto remained unnoticed in the Writings of Geometers. By J. R. Young. 8vo. 8s.

"Mr. Young's observations on the theory of parallel lines, the labour he has bestowed on the doctrine of proportion, as well as his corrections of many errors of preceding geometers, and supplying their defects, together with his minute attention to accuracy throughout, may be justly considered as rendering his performance valuable, especially to the learner."—*Philosophical Magazine, March* 1828.

"In the notes, which he has appended to the volume, is much valuable matter, even for those who have advanced still further in these studies. On the theory of parallel lines, which has not a little perplexed geometers of all ages, there is a very able and elaborate commentary."—*The Times, November* 2, 1827.

"In perspicuity Euclid has no rival, except, perhaps, in that part of his work which treats of geometrical proportion. This is abstruse, and subtle, and intricate. The doctrine of proportion, as connected with geometry, must necessarily be so. Hence Legendre has excluded the consideration of it from his Elements, leaving all knowledge of the subject to be acquired from numerical proportion. This is a defect which Mr. Young has ably supplied. Indeed, we have never seen a work so free from pretension, and of such great merit. Various fallacies latent in the reasonings of some celebrated mathematicians, both of ancient and modern date, are pointed out and discussed in a tone of calm moderation, which we regret to say is not always employed in the scientific world."—*Monthly Magazine.*

2. AN ELEMENTARY TREATISE on ALGEBRA;

Theoretical and Practical; with Attempts to simplify some of the more difficult Parts of the Science, particularly the Demonstration of the Binomial Theorem, in its most general form; the Solution of Equations of the higher orders; the Summation of Infinite Series, &c. A new edition. By J. R. Young. 12mo. cloth. 5s. 6d.

"A new and ingenious general method of solving Equations has been recently discovered by Messrs. H. Atkinson, Holdred, and Horner, independently of each other. For the best practical view of this new method and its applications, consult the elementary Treatise on Algebra, by Mr. J. R. Young, a work which deserves our cordial recommendation."—*Dr. Gregory's edit. of Hutton's Mathematics,* vol. i.

"For the summation of infinite series the author gives a new and ingenious method, which is very easy and extensive in its application."—*Newcastle Magazine.*

3. A KEY to the ABOVE, by W. H. Spiller. 6s.

4. THE GENERAL THEORY and SOLUTION of

ALGEBRAICAL EQUATIONS, in which are embodied the Recent Researches of Budan, Fourier, and Horner; together with a complete

Solution of the Important Problem of the Separation of the Real and Imaginary Roots of an Equation, under all circumstances; being the substance of a remarkable paper by M. Sturm, printed among the Mémoires présentés par divers savans à l'Académie Royale des Sciences de l'Institut de France. By J. R. Young. 12mo. 9s.

"The importance of the subject to mathematical students, the novelty as well as the beauty of the theorems laid down, and the able and luminous manner in which the whole subject has been treated by Professor Young, have induced us to embrace the earliest opportunity of inviting the attention of the scientific portion of our readers to his excellent publication, the title of which sufficiently explains its objects. The improvements and discoveries which the continental analysts have recently made in regard to the methods of resolving general equations, have hitherto been, in a great measure, unknown to the public of Great Britain and Ireland, as is well explained by Professor Young, in the introduction to his work: and when, to this circumstance, we add, the clearness, the elegance, and, at the same time, the profound ability with which that learned gentleman has methodized and discussed his subject, we conceive that we are bestowing upon his labours no undeserved eulogium, when we state, that were we to leave his other numerous and valuable works altogether out of the question, he has, in the one before us, laid the cultivators of science under no common obligation.

"But, however deserved may be the praise which we thus willingly accord to Professor Young, we have another object, as we have already intimated, in noticing his publication; and this object is, first, to draw the attention of mathematicians in this part of the country to one of the most important, as well as the most remarkable discoveries that have been made since the time of Descartes; and, secondly, to correct one or two inaccuracies into which Professor Peacock has fallen, in his very elaborate and valuable report on the recent progress and present state of certain branches of mathematical analysis, published in the account of the proceedings of the third meeting of the British Association.

"The discovery to which we have adverted is fully developed and applied in the seventh chapter of the work before us, entitled 'On the Theorem of Sturm,' a theorem by the aid of which the important problem of the separation of the roots of an equation—a problem which has engaged the attention of the ablest mathematicians for the last two hundred years—is at length completely and satisfactorily solved. We are aware that the possibility of a solution to this great problem was clearly shown by the celebrated Lagrange, first in the Memoirs of Berlin for 1767, and afterwards in his well known work on the 'Resolution des Equations Numériques,' where the steps of the process are fully explained. Such, however, is the vast amount of numerical labour, and the consequent risk of error involved in this process, that, much as it has been admired for its abstract analytical elegance, its entire impracticability has been acknowledged and lamented by all subsequent writers on the subject. For M. Sturm, however, has been reserved the honour of giving perfection to this department of analysis; he has solved the problem in question by a process of very remarkable simplicity, involving but few numerical operations, and those too of the easiest character; and he has thus secured for his name the same distinguished position in the theory of equations, which that of Taylor occupies in the differential calculus.

"We must confess that we were somewhat disappointed at not finding any announcement of Sturm's theorem among the published reports of the recent meeting of the British Association in Dublin.

"We had hoped to have seen it noticed in the form of an addendum to Professor Peacock's account of recent discoveries, alluded to above; which addendum would also have afforded the learned Professor an opportunity of correcting some inadvertencies in his report respecting the researches of Fourier and Budan. We believe, however, that not only the first account of Sturm's theorem, but even the first announcement of it, in the English language, is to be found in the volume before us.

" We need scarcely conclude by adding, that, by the present work, Professor Young
has not only sustained his previous reputation, but has won new claims to public
favour; and, so far as our recommendation may be influential, we can have no
hesitation in bestowing it with the utmost cordiality, as this treatise on the ' *Theory
and Solution of Algebraical Equations*' is one without which every scientific library
must be incomplete.'—*Extracted from the Belfast News-Letter, Oct. 30, 1835.*
⁎ See also *Philosophical Magazine*, May, 1836.

5. ELEMENTS of PLANE and SPHERICAL TRIGO-
NOMETRY, with its Applications to the Principles of Navigation and
Nautical Astronomy, with the necessary Logarithmic and Trigonome-
trical Tables. By J. R. Young. To which is added, some Original
Researches in Spherical Geometry. By T. S. Davies, esq. F.R.S.E.
F.R.A.S. &c. 6s. cloth.

6. MATHEMATICAL TABLES; comprehending the
Logarithms of all Numbers from 1 to 36,000; also the Natural and Logarithmic Sines and Tangents; computed to seven places of Decimals,
and arranged on an improved Plan; with several other Tables, useful
in Navigation and Nautical Astronomy, and in other departments of
Practical Mathematics. By J. R. Young. 6s. 6d. cloth.

7. An ELEMENTARY TREATISE on the COMPUTA-
TION of LOGARITHMS; intended as a Supplement to the various
Books on Algebra. A new edition, enlarged. By J. R. Young. 12mo. 5s.
See Dr. Gregory's edition of Hutton's Mathematics, vol. i. p. 157, where a particu-
lar reference is made to this work.

8. ELEMENTS of ANALYTICAL GEOMETRY, com-
prehending the Doctrine of the Conic Sections, and the general Theory
of Curves and Surfaces of the second order, with a variety of local
Problems on Lines and Surfaces. Intended for the use of Mathematical
Students in Schools and Universities. By J. R. Young. 9s. cloth.

" If works like the present be introduced generally into our schools and colleges, the
Continent will not long boast of its immense superiority over the country of Newton,
in every branch of modern analytical science."—*The Atlas, July 25, 1830.*

9. ELEMENTS of the DIFFERENTIAL CALCULUS;
comprehending the General Theory of Curve Surfaces and of Curves of
Double Curvature. Second Edition. By J. R. Young. 12mo. 9s. in
cloth.

Also an Octavo Edition for the Universities. Price 12s.

" The work is divided into three sections, and each section is subdivided into chapters of a moderate length. The first section treats of the differentiation of functions
in general; the second contains the application of the differential calculus to the
theory of plane curves; and the third unfolds the general theory of curve surfaces and
of curves of double curvature. In the first, the author introduces the most valuable
theorems and formulæ of the celebrated analysts, Euler, Lagrange, Demoivre, and
Cotes. In the second, he has given a correct explanation of what the French have
termed consecutive curves. The third contains the most beautiful theorems of Euler,
Monge, and Dupin, relative to the curvature of surfaces in general, together with a
chapter on twisted surfaces, a subject hitherto confined to foreign writers. The whole
forms a more simple, consistent, and comprehensive view of the differential calculus,
and its various applications, than any hitherto published.

" But the work does not merit attention merely on account of arrangement, and the
judicious selection which it contains from the writings of others. It has also claims

to originality. What the author has adopted from other writers, he has rendered much more simple. The chapter on maxima and minima presents considerable improvements in various parts of the investigation. In surveying the cases in which Taylor's theorem fails, Mr. Young has shown that it does not fail where the coefficients become imaginary, as is asserted by Lacroix and his followers, but that these failing cases are always indicated by the coefficients becoming infinite. In one of the problems on this subject he has detected a false solution by Lagrange, which has been transcribed by Garnier and several others, merely on the faith of a great name.

"The whole Elements of the Differential Calculus, comprehending all that is most valuable in the large works of the most celebrated Analysts, are contained in a duodecimo volume, beautifully printed on a fine paper and neatly bound in cloth. It appears to be in every respect well fitted for a Class Book, and can scarcely fail to be very generally adopted."—*Presbyterian Review.*

"There are no affected changes of method : there is no parade of original plan or of novelty of principle ; and yet there is much original matter, much original reasoning, and, what is of more value than all questions about originality in an elementary treatise, there is a perspicuity, a unity of method prevailing in all its parts, that renders it, more than any book we have seen, *peculiarly adapted to instruction.*

"It is not, however, as an elegant and perspicuous development of the first principles of the Calculus, merely, that we have admired, and therefore recommended Mr. Young's little work ; we have also found much to commend in it of a more profound character ; much that we look for in vain in larger works, and indeed in *all* English books.

"The paralogisms of some other writers, distinguished ones too, are pointed out in the preface, and in the body of the work ; and many steps which have hitherto been deemed unquestionable, have been shewn by Mr. Young to be altogether fallacious. We wonder, indeed, when we see them pointed out, why they did not occur to ourselves nor to any body else till now ; and we look upon the aptitude displayed in these detections to be highly characteristic of a mind which looks with a laudable anxiety to the purity of the fundamental principles of science."—*Philo. Magazine, October* 1831.

10. ELEMENTS of the INTEGRAL CALCULUS ; with its Applications to Geometry, and to the Summation of Infinite Series, &c. By J. R. Young. 9s. in cloth.

"The volume before us forms the third of an Analytical Course, which commences with the ' *Elements of Analytical Geometry.*' More elegant Text-books do not exist in the English Language, and we trust they will speedily be adopted in our Mathematical Seminaries. The existence of such auxiliaries will, of itself, we hope, prove an inducement to the cultivation of Analytical Science ; for, to the want of such Elementary Works, the indifference hitherto manifested in this country on the subject, is, we apprehend, chiefly to be ascribed. Mr. Young has brought the science within the reach of every intelligent student, and, in so doing, has contributed to the advancement of Mathematical Learning in Great Britain."—*Presbyterian Review.*

11. ELEMENTS of MECHANICS ; comprehending the Theory of Equilibrium and of Motion, and the first Principles of Physical Astronomy, together with a variety of Statical and Dynamical Problems. Illustrated by numerous engravings. By J. R. Young. 10s. 6d. in cloth.

"Mr. Young is already favourably known to the public by his writings ; and the Treatise on Mechanics, which we now propose briefly to notice, will add considerably to his reputation as the author of elementary works of science.

"To read the works of Laplace, Ivory, Somerville, &c. a knowledge of the methods employed by these writers is previously required, and renders such preparatory works as those of Mr. Young absolutely necessary.'—*Presbyterian Review.*

12. A LECTURE on the STUDY of the MATHEMATICS. By J. R. Young. 2s. 6d.

1. LACROIX'S ELEMENTS of ALGEBRA ; translated from the French. By W. H. Spiller. 12mo. 7s. 6d.

2. ON THE SOLUTION of NUMERICAL EQUA-TIONS. By C. Sturm. Translated from the Mémoires présentés par divers Savans à l'Académie Royale des Sciences de l'Institut de France. By W. H. Spiller. 4to. Sewed, 7s. 6d.

3. AN ESSAY on MUSICAL INTERVALS, HARMO-NICS, and TEMPERAMENT ; in which the most delicate, interesting, and useful parts of the Theory are explained, in a manner adapted to the comprehension of the practical Musician. By W. S. B. Woolhouse. 12mo. 5s.

4. DIX'S TREATISE on LAND-SURVEYING. 8s.

5. THE ELEMENTS of EUCLID ; first Six Books ; together with the Eleventh and Twelfth. By R. Simpson. 8vo. 9s. bd.; royal 18mo. 7s. 6d. bound.

6. HUTTON's COMPLETE COURSE of MATHEMA-TICS, improved by Dr. Gregory. New edition, Vol. I. 8vo. 12s. bds.

7.   Vol. II. 8vo.

8. ——————— MENSURATION. 12mo. 4s. bound.

9. ——————— KEY to ditto. 12mo. 4s. 6d. bound.

10. A BRIEF TREATISE on the USE and CONSTRUC-TION of a CASE of MATHEMATICAL INSTRUMENTS ; contain-ing a copious Explanation of each, particularly of the Sector, the lines of which are separately treated of, and their use shewn in solving seve-ral cases of Trigonometry ; the whole designed to give the young Stu-dent a knowledge in using his instruments, and constructing geometri-cal figures with accuracy. By George Phillips, B.A., Queen's College, Cambridge. New edition. 2s. 6d.

GENERAL SCIENCE.

1. AN INTRODUCTION to the ARTS and SCIENCES. By R. Turner. 18mo. 4s. bound.

2. THE SOLAR SYSTEM ; arranged in a new and fami-liar manner, so as to enable Youth to comprehend more clearly the relative Magnitudes and Distances of its Parts. By R. W. 6d.
For a character of this little work, see *Mechanics' Magazine*, *Oct.* 1824.

3. INSTRUCTIONS for the MIXTURE of WATER-COLOURS, for Miniature, Landscape, Flower, and Fruit Painting ; with the Elements of Painting in Water-Colours : treated in a manner calculated to render the whole easy of attainment to every capacity. Third Edition, improved. By H. Harrison, Professor of Painting. 2s. 6d.

4. SYMONS'S PRACTICAL GAUGER. 12mo. 7s.

MORAL.

1. INFANTINE STORIES; in Words of One, Two, and Three Syllables. By Mrs. Fenwick. With six copper-plate Engravings. 2s. and 3s. coloured.

This is one of the most interesting little Books that can be put into the hands of a child, after Clark's excellent little Primer.

2. MORNINGS in the LIBRARY. By Ann Knight. With Introductory Lines and Concluding Poem, by Bernard Barton. 18mo. 2s. 6d.

3. MORE MINOR MORALS. By Aunt Eleanor. 12mo. 3s. 6d.

4. CHARLES and EUGENIA. 12mo. 4s.

5. LADY ANN. By the Author of " The Blue Silk Work-Bag." 18mo. 2s. 6d.

6. TALES for MY PUPILS. 18mo. 2s. 6d.

7. SIX MORAL TALES for YOUTH; from the French of Madame Genlis. Royal 18mo. 3s.

8. THE PUZZLE for a CURIOUS GIRL: a new and very superior Edition, revised and enlarged; with all the copperplate Engravings the full size of the page. 2s. and 3s. coloured.

9. THE SCHOOLFELLOWS; a Moral and Instructive Tale for Girls. By Miss Sandham, Author of the " Twin Sisters," " Bee and Butterfly," &c. 18mo. 3s.

10. THE BOY'S SCHOOL; or, Traits of Character in Early Life. A Moral Tale, by the same. 3s.

11. BLOSSOMS of MORALITY. 18mo. 2s. 6d.

12. SACRED and MISCELLANEOUS POETRY, by M. A. P. 18mo. 2s. 6d. half-bound.

13. ROBINSON CRUSOE, complete. Two vols. in one, with Plates. 4s. 6d. boards, or 5s. half-bound.

RELIGIOUS.

1. BIBLE LETTERS for CHILDREN, by Lucy Barton. With Introductory Verses by Bernard Barton. In 1 vol. 18mo., fine paper and type, with frontispiece. 3s. half-bound; also a Cheap Edition for Schools. 2s.

"We think this little volume does infinite credit to the youthful writer. The selections are very judicious; and the lessons dwelt upon and explained in a simple manner, obvious to the most juvenile capacity."—*Literary Gazette*, August 27, 1831.

"This is one of the best books for young persons that we have seen for a long time. The style is very easy and natural, and the whole work excellent."
Home Missionary, September 1, 1831.

"Although we do not often notice books of this class, we have great pleasure in recommending this, as one that will become a favorite."—*New Monthly Magazine*, Oct. 1, 1831.

"We almost envy the parent whose young daughter has talent and grace sufficient to enable her to write such letters as these for the rising generation."—*Evangelical Magazine*, Oct. 1, 1831.

"Parents will find this volume well suited for interesting and instructing the juvenile branches of their families."—*World*, August 22, 1831.

"On looking into the work, we meet that which we expected to find, chastity of style, purity and simplicity of thought, combined with a truly Christian code of morality."—*Spectator*, Sept. 10, 1831.

"Unlike too many books intended for children, the style of these letters is not above their comprehension, whilst simplicity is kept free from meanness."—*Athenæum*, Sept. 17, 1831.

"Lucy Barton has gently and gracefully descended to the level of her youthful readers: she first awakens their attention by a well-chosen history, she then satisfies the judgment by a judicious reflection, or touches the heart by an affecting appeal."—*Suffolk Chronicle*, Sept. 3, 1831.

"We have been greatly pleased both with the plan and execution of this unpretending little volume. Miss Barton has judiciously adopted the epistolary form, as best allied in its structure to that simplicity of composition which is one of the distinguishing features of her great original."—*Ipswich Journal*, Sept. 3, 1831.

"Children's books on religious topics should be catholic in the truest sense of the word; and, as might reasonably be expected, these Bible Letters have nothing sectarian in them, but are such as any parent, of any religious denomination, may put into the hands of his child."—*Friends' Magazine*, 9th Month, 1831.

"This is an admirable little volume, and deserves the especial regard of parents and teachers."—*Carlisle Patriot*, Sept. 17, 1831.

2. BIBLE QUESTIONS; a plain, easy, and inviting Assistance to the Study of the Holy Scriptures. For the Use of Schools and Families. By W. Humble, of Exeter College, Oxford. Part I., the OLD TESTAMENT; Part II., the NEW TESTAMENT. Each 2s. 6d. in cloth.

3. BARBAULD'S HYMNS, in prose. 18mo. 1s. Large letter, 1s. 6d. 12mo., with cuts, 3s. half-bound.

4. WATTS'S DIVINE and MORAL SONGS for Children, embellished with beautiful Engravings. The best Edition printed. 18mo. 6d. half-bound.

5. WATTS'S FIRST SET OF CATECHISMS AND PRAYERS. Best Edition printed. 24mo., fine. 2d. sewed.

6. WATTS'S SECOND SET of CATECHISMS and PRAYERS. 24mo. fine. 4d. sewed.

7. WATTS'S FIRST and SECOND SETS, bound together. 9d.

8. A CATECHISM, DRAWN from the PENTA-TEUCH; intended to illustrate that part of Sacred Writ, and to familiarise it to the minds of the rising Generation. By J. H. 1s. 6d. bound.

9. WATTS'S VIEW of the WHOLE SCRIPTURE HISTORY, by Question and Answer. 12mo. 1s. bound.

10. AN INTRODUCTION to the KNOWLEDGE of the CHRISTIAN RELIGION, by H. Crossman, M.A. Rector of Little Bromley, Essex. A new Edition, large type. 1s. neatly bound.

11. SECKER'S (Abp.) LECTURES on the CHURCH CATECHISM. 12mo. 4s.; 8vo. 9s.

12. THE COLLECTS for the SUNDAYS and HOLI-DAYS throughout the YEAR; with Forms of Prayer, and the Catechism of the Church of England. 4d., or 3s. 4d. per dozen, and 24s. per hundred.

13. THE CATECHISM separately, 3d.   The COLLECTS separately, 2d.

As these Collects and Catechisms are printed from a clear type, and on a very superior paper, it is necessary to order Souter's Editions.

MISCELLANEOUS.

1. MEMOIR of HENRY PESTALOZZI, and his PLAN of EDUCATION: being an account of his Life and Writings, with copious Extracts from his Works, and extensive details illustrative of the practical parts of his Method. By E. Biber, Ph. Dr. 8vo. 14s. cloth.

2. A BIOGRAPHICAL DICTIONARY, by Stephen Jones: new Edition, with nearly Three Hundred additional Names. 18mo. 6s. bound.

3. TRUSLER'S DOMESTIC MANAGEMENT; or the Art of Conducting a Family with Economy, Frugality, and Method; the result of long experience. With full instructions to servants, of various denominations, how to time their work well. New Edition. 12mo. 5s.

4. A PERPETUAL KEY to the ALMANACKS, with an Explanation of the Astronomical and Chronological Terms. By James Bannantine. 2s. 6d.

INTRODUCTORY FRENCH BOOKS.

1. THE NEW FRENCH PRIMER; containing a Vocabulary of familiar Words and Phrases, arranged in the most pleasing Form; on one page are easy words, illustrated by engravings; and in the following page the same words occur again, formed into short sentences. And to which are annexed, interesting Dialogues, in which the name of almost every article in domestic use, whether of furniture, of dress, or for the breakfast or dinner table is introduced. The whole illustrated by upwards of Two Hundred and Fifty Engravings. By Mad. Douin. 1s.

2. CATECHISME D'UNE MERE; pour les Enfans. Contenant les choses les plus nécessaires à connaitre dans l'Enfance. Destiné à servir de suite au Vocabulaire. Par Mad. Douin. With One Hundred Engravings. 1s. sewed.

3. FIRST FRENCH GRAMMAR, in Question and Answer, by A. Gombert; with Exercises on the Rules, by J. C. Tarver, French Professor at Eton College. Price 9d. sewed, or 1s. bound.

4. L'ABEILLE. A FIRST BOOK for translating French into English. By E. A. Mansart; a new edition, revised by the Author of Le Nouveau Tresor, and intended as a sequel to the above Grammar. 18mo. 1s.

5. LE NOUVEAU TRESOR, or French Student's Companion; designed to facilitate the Translation of English into French at Sight, and at the same time to convey Instruction in Science, Literature, and Morality. Fourth Edition, with Additions, and an Introduction to French Grammar. By M, E*** S*****. 3s. neatly bound.

6. THE BOOK of VERSIONS; or, Guide to French Translation and Construction. By J. Cherpilloud, Professor of the French Language at the Royal Military College, Sandhurst. Revised, corrected, and improved. 12mo. 3s. 6d.

This Book is intended to facilitate the Translation of English into French, and to assist the Pupil in the construction of the French Language: it should be put into his hands as soon as he is acquainted with a few of the principal grammatical rules, in order to lead him to their application. The Book of Versions is divided into easy portions or lessons, which ascend, as to difficulty, in regular gradation. The Notes accompanying each are constructed on the same principle, and furnish the Idioms as well as the Prepositions belonging to Verbs. In this respect, it is presumed they will be essentially serviceable, by forcing a continual comparison between the peculiarities of the two Languages, as displayed in their most characteristic phraseology. The latter part of the Book of Versions contains some specimens of French Poetry from leading Authors, with free Translations.

7. PARTIE FRANCAISE du LIVRE de VERSIONS; ou, Guide à la Traduction de l' Anglais en Français: consisting of elegant Extracts from the best French Classics, &c. 3s. 6d.

FRENCH CLASS BOOKS, BY M. TARVER.

PRINTED FOR   THE USE OF

ETON   COLLEGE,

AND THE ROYAL MILITARY COLLEGE, WOOLWICH.

1. INTRODUCTION à LA LANGUE USUELLE ET AUX ELEMENTS DE LA GRAMMAIRE FRANÇAISE; or Early Introduction to the most common Idioms of French Conversation, and to the Elements of French Grammar; with appropriate Easy and Familiar Exercises. 3s. neatly bound and lettered.

2. FAMILIAR AND CONVERSATIONAL FRENCH EXERCISES for Writing and Viva-Voce Practice; preceded by Tables and Rules on the Grammar and Syntax, and followed by Vocabularies and Dialogues on the common topics of daily Conversation. 3s. 6d.

A KEY to the above. By the same. 12mo. bound. 3s.

3. PHRASEOLOGIE comparée, arrangée Alphabétiquement, pour aider à rendre en Anglais les passages remarquables ou difficiles, sous le rapport de la Grammaire et de la Construction, et les Idiotismes qui se trouvent dans le cours de l'ouvrage; et destinée, en même tems, à servir de Leçons pratiques de conversation. Separate, 3s.

4. CHOIX EN PROSE ET EN VERS, à l'Usage de ceux de MM. les Elèves d'Eton qui apprennent le Français; suivi de la Phraséologie Comparée, et précédé d'un Traité Concis de Versification. By the same. 7s. 6d. neatly bound and lettered.

1ere Partie.—*Prose.* Gil Blas à Valladolid—Charles XII. à Bender—Descente de Télémaque aux Enfers—Histoire de Léo, tirée de Numa Pompilius—Quatre premiers livres des Aventures de Don Quichotte—Scènes Historiques et Nationales ; Mort de Louis XVI., Passage du Niémen, Retraite de la Grande Armée, Chute de Napoléon, Prise de Paris, Spectacles de Paris, Cour des Messageries ; tirées de Mignet, Segur, Jouy, et du Livre des Cent et un—Scènes de la Manie de Briller, la Petite Ville, les Ricochets de Picard.—200 pp.

2de Partie.— *Vers.* Vingt Fables, tirées de Florian, La Fontaine, et autres—Second et troisième Chants de la Henriade—de l'Homme, Huitième Satire de Boileau—Second Chant des Jardins, de Delille—Fragment de Sédim, ou les Nègres, de Viennet—Poésies Lyriques, tirées de Voltaire ; J. B. Rousseau ; Lambert ; A. de La Martine ; Hugo ; C. Delavigne ; Clotilde de Surville ; Mérope, tragédie de Voltaire—Troisième Scènes de Charles VII. chez ses grands Vasseaux, tragédie de Dumas.

3e Partie. La Phraséologie Comparée, arrangée Alphabétiquement, pour aider à rendre en Anglais les passages remarquables ou difficiles, sous le rapport 'de la Grammaire et de la Construction, et 'les Idiotismes, qui se trouvent dans le cours de l'ouvrage ; et destinée, en même tems, à servir de Leçons pratiques de conversation.

"We think Mr. Tarver's publication the best we have seen to meet the wants of English learners. He does not offer it as a manual for self-instruction. In fact, no scheme of learning a language can be more absurd than that which proceeds without the assistance of a native. But, as a guide and a help both to teacher and learner, this volume seems to us to supply in principle all that can be desired."—*Berkshire Chronicle.*

"Mr. Tarver, French Master of Eton College, is already advantageously known to the public as the writer of some excellent Works on the French language, and the volume before us is well calculated to increase his celebrity. It must have occurred to every one, that in instruction nothing is more ennuyeuse, both to teacher and pupil, than the constant recurrence to, and the continually plodding through, one tedious interminable volume, be it ever so exquisitely written. This idea has forced itself upon the author of the work before us, who observes, in illustration of it, ' I have known people unable to surmount their disgust for Télémaque, because it had been the book used by them to learn French.' In remedying this defect, however, he has not fallen into the opposite extreme of collecting together a multiplicity of meagre and unconnected scraps, which, from their extreme brevity, would be incapable of fixing attention, much less of creating anything like interest. Mr. Tarver has happily hit upon the golden mean, and avoided both extremes. His work is after the manner of our ' Elegant Extracts in Prose and Verse,' and, without reference to tuition, is a remarkably interesting selection. Besides pieces from the old French classics, it embraces portions of the most interesting works of celebrated modern French writers, such as Mignet's French Revolution, Count Segur's History of the Russian War, and extracts from the writings of Jouy, Picard, Bazin, Delavigne, &c. &c. thus not only placing before the reader the best specimens of the modern French style, but making him acquainted, at the same time, with the manners and customs of our interesting neighbours. One important feature of Mr. Tarver's work we had almost forgotten to notice ; it is that which is styled ' Phraséologie Expliquée.' This portion of the work is devoted to a comparison between the phraseology of the two languages, to show where they differ in construction, and to point out the frequent variance between the same words in their French and English acceptation. An example or two will more clearly explain our meaning. The author observes, ' it would be wofully wrong to render the English sentence— *He is very ill, we sat up all night with him,* by—*Il est bien malade,* nous sommes assis toute la nuit auprès de lui, instead of—*Nous l'avons veillé toute la nuit.* Again, *my trouble* and *mon trouble* are by no means convertible terms—the former means *ma peine,* and the latter *my confusion.*' We can conscientiously recommend the work to our readers, and have no doubt of its finding a prominent place among the best standard school-books. We perceive that it is dedicated to the young Prince of Cambridge, whom Mr. Tarver has the honour to instruct.'—*Windsor and Eton Express.*

"The Phraséologie Comparée will be found of essential service to the learner in the attainment of a knowledge of the respective idioms of the two languages, and the well selected extracts from the French writers, ancient and modern, are not only calculated to forward the student in his pursuits, but convey correct and useful ideas of the manners and customs of the French at the present day, thus supplying a *desideratum* long wanted in this branch of education."—*Macclesfield Courier & Herald, April 15, 1833.*

"It is a most judicious and comprehensive selection from various esteemed French writers, exemplifying the varieties of their style, in most amusing and attractive extracts ; and thus supplying a French class-book for reading in schools, which is both diversified and valuable."—*The Annalist, April 1833.*

5. DICTIONNAIRE DES VERBES FRANÇAIS ;

showing the Case and Mood which they require after them. Second Edition. By the same. 400 pages, 7s. boards.

"In the present day, when French is so universally spoken, every assistance towards vanquishing its difficulties and acquiring its fluency must be readily welcomed, and the volume now before us is well calculated to advance and assist the student. M. Tarver has collected and arranged the *idioms* in a clear and perspicuous manner. We cordially recommend this work as a valuable aid to the learner of that necessary language, the French."—*Literary Gazette.*

FRENCH WORKS, BY M. DE ROUILLON.

1. AN INTRODUCTION to the STUDY of the FRENCH LANGUAGE; or, a Vocabulary of the most useful Nouns, Adjectives, and Verbs: together with a Series of Elementary Sentences. 2s. 6d.

2. ABREGE de l'HISTOIRE SAINTE, à l'Usage de la Jeunesse. 18mo. 9d. sewed.

3. ABREGE de l'HISTOIRE ANCIENNE de la GRECE. 3s.

4. INSTITUTIONS de MORALE, à l'Usage de la Jeunesse. Nouvelle Edition, revué et corrigée. 2s. 6d.

5. GRAMMATICAL INSTITUTES of the French Language; or, the Teacher's French Assistant: containing a Series of Theoretical, Practical, and Progressive Lessons, in which every difficulty is explained. New Edition. 5s. neatly bound and lettered.

6. EXERCISES on FRENCH CONVERSATION, or a Selection of English Sentences to be translated into French. 3s. 6d.

7. A KEY to Ditto. 1s. 6d.

8. A SEQUEL to the EXERCISES on FRENCH CONVERSATION: a Selection of English Pieces to be translated into French, forming a Complement to every Grammar, and especially intended to remove the Difficulties in the use of the perfect and imperfect Tenses of French Verbs. 4s. 6d.—A KEY to Ditto. 3s.

9. A COMPLETE ANALYTICAL TABLE of the GENDERS of all the FRENCH NOUNS, by which one of the greatest Difficulties of the French Language is entirely removed. New Edition. 8vo. 3s. 6d.

10. VOYAGE de POLYCLETE, ou LETTRES ROMAINES, abrégé de l'Ouvrage original de M. le Baron de Theis, à l'usage de la Jeunesse. New Edition, improved. 12mo. 7s. bound.

" This little work, in the interesting form of letters from a young Greek, is a compendium of information respecting the Habits, Manners, and Customs of the Romans, not only at the period of which it more particularly treats, but also, by means of apt and ingenious digressive allusions, to the earlier days of that once mighty people.

" After the sacking of Atheus by Sylla, in his Mithridatic expedition, Polycletas, son of the Archon, Crantor, becomes a hostage for the Athenian good behaviour, and is sent to Rome: there he is generously received, as a fallen enemy of rank, into the house of the Consul L. Octavius, by whose kindness a well-informed and privileged slave is assigned to him as cicerone. In company with this intelligent person, he explores Rome, comments upon every thing he sees, and repeats all that he hears connected with the people and the city, in a series of letters to his friends at Athens; and after being an eyewitness to many occurrences possessing considerable historical interest, during those stirring times when Marius and Sylla figured so conspicuously on the same scene together, he is eventually released from his half-bondage, half-tourist state, by order of the Dictator, in return for having discovered and revealed a plot against his life. This epoch, thus judiciously chosen, naturally leads to the

introduction of many personages who occupied important stations in the eye of the
world at the time; and affords favorable scope, of which due advantage is taken, for
conveying information respecting the civil and religious policy, and the domestic
arrangements of the Romans.

"The work before us may fairly take rank, without fear from comparison, with
the well-known abridgment of the Abbé Barthelemi's 'Travels of Anacharsis the
Younger,' and which we decidedly consider a valuable appendage to School Libraries
With this intention on the part of the translator, the son of Crantor is sent forth
in a cheap dress; and while we recommend him as a very eligible companion for our
juvenile friends, we can assure their parents that they themselves need not disdain to
scrape acquaintance with the young Athenian, who will be found an agreeable and
entertaining companion." *London University Mag.*, Jan. 1, 1830.

11. MYTHOLOGIE des DEMOISELLES, ou Abrégé de
l'Histoire Poétique des Dieux et des Héros. Par M. de Rouillon.
6s. 6d.

THE SYSTEMS OF HAMILTON AND JACOTOT UNITED AND IMPROVED.

1. A GRAMMAR of the FRENCH LANGUAGE, for
English Students, upon a plan entirely original. By S. Brookes. Author of the Analytical Translation of Petit Jack, Elisabeth, and Telemaque, &c. 12mo. 2s. 6d.

2. PETIT JACK. By the Author of Sandford and Mer-
ton, arranged for Students commencing the French Language; with an
Analytical Translation in the order of the Text; the Pronunciation
indicated according to the best French Authorities; distinguishing the
Silent Letters, Nasal Sounds, and other Irregularities; Explanatory
Notes, and an Alphabetical Reference to all the words made use of.
By S. B. 3s. 6d.

A Small Edition, French only, 18mo. 1s. bound.

3. ELISABETH, ou LES EXILES de SIBERIE, de Mad.
de Cottin, arranged for Students commencing the study of the French
Language; with an Analytical Translation in the order of the Text;
the Pronunciation indicated according to the best French Authorities;
Explanatory Notes, and an Alphabetical Reference to all the words made
use of, &c., on the same plan as Petit Jack. By S. B. 5s.

4. THE FIRST SIX BOOKS of TELEMAQUE, arranged
on the same plan as Petit Jack and Elisabeth. By S. B. 5s. 6d.

5. NEW and ENTERTAINING DIALOGUES, in French
andEnglish, on an improved Interlinear System, &c., adapted to the Hamiltonian System. Second Edition. By J. F. Gerard, M.A. 4s. in cloth.

"This work professes to render the acquirement of the French Language less a
matter of dull monotonous study than of amusement. The mode adopted for fami
liarising the student with the genders, by the arrangement of the first and last letters,
is simple and ingenious, and has, we believe, the advantage of novelty to recommend
it."—*Court Journal*, No. 120.

6. EDGEWORTH'S FRANK, prepared as a Course of
FRENCH EXERCISES, adapted to the System of M. Jacotot, in two
parts. 1s. 6d. sewed.

THE HAMILTONIAN SYSTEM.

This System has been pronounced, by the Edinburgh Review, " one of the most useful and important discoveries of the age," and by the Westminster Review, " the most extraordinary improvement in the Method of Instruction which the ingenuity of the human mind has hitherto devised." This Review also ascribes to the Author of the Hamiltonian System, exclusively, " the great merit of introducing Translations, made in invariable accordance with a principle of a strict verbal analysis;" and it remarks, that " it is this peculiarity which renders them such invaluable instruments to the learner."

LATIN.	s.	d.	FRENCH.	s.	d.
Gospel of St. John, in cloth	4	0	Elisabeth, or the Exiles of		
Epitome Historiæ Sacræ ..	4	0	Siberia	5	0
Æsop's Fables	4	0	Florian's Fables, 12mo. cloth	5	0
Phædrus' Fables..........	4	0	Frank, 2 Parts	1	6
Eutropius	4	0	Gospel of St. John, in cloth	4	0
Aurelius Victor	4	0	Perrin's Fables	5	0
Cornelius Nepos	6	6	Recueil Choisi	7	6
Selectæ è Profanis, 2 vol. ..	13	0	Telemachus	5	0
Cæsar's Commentaries	7	6	Verbs	2	0
Celsus de Medicina, 3 vols.					
12mo. cloth*	20	0	GERMAN.		
Cicero's Four Orations,12mo.			Edward in Scotland	4	6
cloth	4	0	Gospel of St. John	4	0
Gregory's Conspectus Medi-			Robinson der Jungere, 2 vol.	10	0
cina, 2 vols. 12mo. cloth..	16	0			
Latin Verbs, second Edition	2	0	ITALIAN.		
Sallust	7	6	Gospel of St. John	4	0
First Six books of the Æneid	9	0	Merope, by Alfieri	5	0
Ovid	7	6	Notti Romane	6	6
GREEK.			Novelle Morali	4	0
Gospel of St. John........	6	0	Raccolta di Favole	5	6
Gospel of St. Matthew	7	6	Tasso's Jerusalem Delivered	5	6
Æsop's Fables	6	0	Verbs	2	0
Analecta Minora	6	0			
Aphorisms of Hippocrates,			SPANISH.		
12mo.	9	0	Gospel of St. John	4	0

The HISTORY, PRINCIPLES, PRACTICE, and RESULTS of the
Hamiltonian System, from its Origin to this Time; with
Mr. Hamilton's Lecture at Liverpool, and his Answers
to the Edinburgh and Westminster Reviews 1 6

* Any of the Eight Books may be had separately, price 2s. sewed; and
the Latin Text of the whole, in one volume, 6s. in cloth.

THE FRENCH DRAMA,

ILLUSTRATED BY ARGUMENTS IN ENGLISH AT THE HEAD OF
EACH SCENE;

WITH NOTES, CRITICAL AND EXPLANATORY,
BY A. GOMBERT.

UNDER this title the best productions of the French Dramatic writers
are in course of publication, each play elucidated—

1st. BY APPROPRIATE ARGUMENTS at the head of each scene, to
unravel the plot, as well as develop the subject, characters, and various
incidents throughout the piece.

2d. BY AN ENGLISH TRANSLATION of such words and idioms as
may arrest the progress of the reader.

3d. BY CRITICAL OBSERVATIONS, in which will be interspersed
occasional remarks upon the beauties of the style and conceptions.

The Drama, that exquisite and invaluable portion of French literature, cannot fail to present many perplexities. By the different
illustrations given, it will be seen that the chief object is to render the
path easy and pleasant, and to unfold beauties of the scene which might
otherwise lie unobserved or unregarded.

The selection embraces the high and dignified character of Tragedy,
as well as the refined and spirited elegance of the Comic Muse.

COMEDIES, BY
MOLIERE.

1. Le Misanthrope,	8. Les Precieuses Ridicules,
2. L'Avare,	9. L'Écoles des Femmes,
3. Le Bourgeois Gentilhomme,	10. L'Écoles des Maris,
4. Le Tartuffe,	11. Le Médecin Malgré Lui,
5. Le Malade Imaginaire,	12. M. de Pourceaugnac,
6. Les Femmes Savantes,	13. Amphitryon.
7. Les Fourberies de Scapin,	

TRAGEDIES, &c. BY
RACINE.

1. La Thébaïde, ou les Frères Ennemis,	7. Bajazet,
	8. Mithridate,
2. Alexandre le Grand,	9. Iphigénie,
3. Andromaque,	10. Phèdre,
4. Les Plaideurs, (Com.)	11. Esther,
5. Britannicus,	12. Athalie.
6. Bérénice,	

TRAGEDIES, &c. BY
P. CORNEILLE.

1. Le Cid,	9. Don Sanche D'Aragon, (Com.)
2. Horace,	10. Nichomède,
3. Cinna,	11. Sertorius,
4. Polyeucte,	
5 Le Menteur, (Com.)	BY T. CORNEILLE.
6. Pompée,	
7. Rodogune,	12. Ariane,
8. Héraclius, Empereur d'Orient,	13. Le Comte D'Essex,
	14. Le Festin de Pierre, (Com.)

VOLTAIRE.

1. Brutus,	4. Mahomet,
2. Zaire,	5. Merope,
3. Alzire,	6. La Mort de César.

To enable persons to make their own selections the Publisher will continue to
sell the plays separately at 1s. each, and 1s. 6d. half-bound, or Moliere, Racine, and
Corneille may be had each in 3 vol. neatly bound, embossed, and gilt edges 15s.

MISCELLANEOUS FRENCH BOOKS.

1. ANTHOLOGIE FRANCAISE; or, selections from the most eminent Poets of France. Second edition, considerably improved, with many additional Notes. By C. Thurgar, Norwich. 6s. 6d.

This compilation, including selections from the most eminent productions of the Augustan age, as well as from the subsequent and living poets of France, may justly claim admission into the Library, or adoption as a Class Book in Schools. The most scrupulous care has been taken to exclude every thing incompatible with delicacy, the object being to unite with intellectual amusement, a course of *religious and moral instruction*.

Pieces of too great length have been abridged, but in a manner to sustain the connexion, and include all that is essential to the interest of the poem. Copious Notes are appended, explaining such passages or allusions as may require elucidation.

2. A NEW THEORETICAL AND HIGHLY PRAC-TICAL FRENCH GRAMMAR; containing numerous graduated colloquial Exercises, on a plan peculiarly conducive to the Speaking of the French Language. By C. J. Delille. Second edit. 12mo., 5s. 6d. bd.

3. LE MANUEL ETYMOLOGIQUE; or, an Interpretative Index of the most recurrent Words in the French Language, exhibiting and illustrating the Roots of those invariable Parts of Speech called Prepositions, Adverbs, and Conjunctions. By C. J. Delille. New edition, 12mo., 2s. 6d.

4. PETIT REPERTOIRE LITTERAIRE; or, miscellaneous Selections in the French Language, from the best French authors of the two last centuries, and from the most distinguished writers of the present day. With numerous illustrations and explanatory notes. By C. J. Delille. 12mo. 5s. 6d. bound.

5. PORNY'S SPELLING, 2s. GRAMMAR, 12mo. 4s. EXERCISES, 2s. 6d.

6. PERRIN'S SPELLING, 2s. FABLES, 2s. 6d. CON-VERSATION, 1s. 6d. GRAMMAR, 4s. EXERCISES, 3s. 6d.

7. DES CARRIERE'S FRENCH PHRASES. 3s. 6d.

8. ——————— HISTOIRE DE FRANCE. 6s. 6d.

9. MAUROIS' MODERN CONVERSATION. 3s. 6d.

10. THE SCHOLAR'S FIRST BOOK. By Ph. le Breton, M.A. 12mo. 3s.

11. SPELLING-BOOK. By Sarah Wanostrocht. 12mo. 2s.

12. A GRAMMAR of the FRENCH LANGUAGE. By D. Wanostrocht. New edition, 12mo. 4s. 6d.

13. FRENCH GRAMMAR. By J. Palairet. 12mo. 4s.

14. L'ABEILLE; a First Book for translating French into English. By E. A. Mansart. New edition, 18mo. 1s.

15. DIALOGUES sur les BEAUX ARTS et LITERA-TURE. Par E. A. Mansart. 2s.

16. DU SUBLIME et des TROPES ; ou, des differents sens dans lesquels on peut prendre un même mot dans une même langue. Par E. A. Mansart. 2s.

17. THE CHAMELEON ; or, Conversations on Every-day Subjects, in French and English; for Young Persons. By F. M. square 12mo. 3s.

18. AVENTURES de TELEMAQUE. Avec les Mots que sont les plus difficiles en Anglais. Par D. Wanostrocht. 12mo. 4s. 6d.

19. NUMA POMPILIUS. Par Florian, avec des Notes par D. Wanostrocht. 12mo. 5s.

20. GIL BLAS. Par le Sage. Abrégé par D. Wanostrocht. 12mo. 6s.

21. BELISAIRE; par M. Marmontel. Avec des Notes par Wanostrocht. 12mo. 4s. 6d.

22. PIERRE LE GRAND. Abrégé par D. Wanostrocht. 5s.

23. CHARLES DOUZE. Abrégé par M. Catty. 12mo. 4s.

24. LA HENRIADE. Par Voltaire. 18mo. 3s. 6d.

25. PIECES CHOISIES de l'AMI des ENFANS. De M. Berquin à l'Usage des Ecoles. 12mo. 4s. 6d.

26. RECUEIL CHOISI de TRAITS HISTORIQUES et des CONTES MORAUX. Par D. Wanostrocht. 12mo. 3s.

27. POESIES de BOILEAU DESPREAUX, avec des Notes, Historiques et Grammaticales. Par M. de Levizac. 12mo. 6s.

28. LECONS FRANCAISES de LITTERATURE et de MORALE. Par M. Noel et M. de la Place. 8vo. 7s.

29. MANUEL EPISTOLAIRE; or, Young Ladies' Assistant in Writing French Letters. 12mo. 6s.

30. KEY to the MANUEL EPISTOLAIRE. 12mo. 3s. 6d.

31. FRENCH DICTIONARY, by J. Nugent. Improved by J. C. Tarver, Professor at Eton College. 18mo. 5s. 6d.

32. A NEW FRENCH DICTIONARY, by J. Nugent. In larger type. square 12mo. 7s. 6d.

33. BOYER'S and DELETANVILLE'S FRENCH and ENGLISH DICTIONARY, united and improved by D. Boileau and A. Picquot. 8vo. 14s.

34. BOTTARELLI'S and POLIDORI'S ENGLISH, FRENCH, and ITALIAN DICTIONARY. 3 vols. 12mo. 21s. bds.

35. DICTIONNAIRE des SYNONYMES. Par M. Levizac. 12mo. bound. 6s. 6d.

36. ABREGE de la BIBLIOTHEQUE PORTATIVE et du PETIT PARNASSE FRANCAIS. Par MM. Levizac, Moysant, &c. square 12mo. 5s.

37. DON QUICHOTTE de la MANCHE, traduit de l'Espagnol, par Florian. Abridged and adapted for the Use of Schools. With Notes by M. Gombert. 12mo. with head of Cervantes. 5s. bound.

38. PETIT JACK. 18mo. bound. 1s.

39. LA CHAUMIERE INDIENNE. Par Jacques Bernardine Henri de St. Pierre. 1s.

40. ALEXANDRE MACLEOD. 18mo. Price 1s.

41. GONSALVE de CORDOUE, ou GRENADE RECONQUISE. Par Florian. New Edition, with Notes. 12mo. 6s.

ITALIAN BOOKS.

1. NOVELLE MORALI. Di Francesco Soave. New Edition, with interlineal and literal Translation. Adapted to the Hamiltonian System. 4s. cloth.

2. LE NOTTI ROMANE del CONTE ALESSANDRO VERRI, al SEPOLCRO DEGLI SCIPIONI. With an interlineal and literal translation. Adapted to the Hamiltonian System. By Mrs. Underwood, daughter of the late Mr. Hamilton: accompanied by Classical and Explanatory Notes by Mr. Underwood. 6s. 6d.

3. TASSO'S JERUSALEM DELIVERED, the First Four Cantos, with an Interlineal and Literal Translation; to which is added, an Explanation of the Practical Sciences. By E. de Rouillon. 18mo. cloth, 5s. 6d.

4. MEROPE: a Tragedy. By Alfieri. With an analytical and interlineal Translation. Adapted to the Hamiltonian System. By Mrs. Merington, daughter of the late Mr. Hamilton, and his assistant in most of his publications. 5s.

5. AN ITALIAN and ENGLISH GRAMMAR, from Vergani's Italian and French Grammar, simplified in twenty Lessons; with Exercises, Dialogues, and entertaining Historical Anecdotes. Corrected and improved by Piranesi, Member of the Academy at Rome; arranged in English and Italian, with Notes, Remarks, and Additions, calculated to facilitate the study of the Italian Language. A new Edition, with very considerable corrections, by M. Guichet. 5s.

6. A KEY, answering to the French and Italian Grammar, as well as to the above. By the same Author. 3s.

7. THE COMPLETE ITALIAN MASTER. By Veneroni. 12mo. 6s.

8. EXERCISES on the DIFFERENT PARTS of ITA-
LIAN SPEECH, with References to Veneroni's Grammar. By F. Bottarelli, A.M. 3s. 6d.—KEY to ditto. By P. R. Rota. 2s. 6d.

9. BARRETTI'S ITALIAN DICTIONARY. 8vo. 26s. bds.

10. BOTTARELLI'S ITALIAN, FRENCH, and ENG-
LISH DICTIONARY. 3 vols. square 12mo. 21s.

11. A NEW GRAMMAR of the ITALIAN LAN-
GUAGE, on a simple and easy plan. By G. A. Graglia. 6s.

12. A NEW POCKET DICTIONARY of the ITALIAN
and ENGLISH LANGUAGES; in two Parts. I. Italian and English :
II. English and Italian. By G. A. Graglia. 7s.

13. SANTAGNELLO'S ITALIAN GRAMMAR. A new
Edition, improved and enlarged. 12mo. 6s. 6d.

14. ——————— EXERCISES to ditto. 12mo. 3s. 6d.

15. ——————— SEQUEL, or New Set of Exercises.
12mo. 4s. 6d.—KEY to the above. 4s. 6d.

16. SANTAGNELLO'S ELIZABETTA. 12mo. 6s. boards.

ITALIAN BOOKS, BY R. ZOTTI.

1. GRAMMAIRE FRANCAISE ET ITALIENNE DE
VENERONI, corrigée, et augmentée d'un Cours de Thèmes, etc. par
R. Zotti. New Edition, 2 vols. 12mo. bound in one, 10s. 6d.

2. CLEF DE LA SUSDITE GRAMMAIRE, pour ceux
qui désirent en traduire les Thèmes d'eux-mêmes, 12mo. bound, 3s.

3. A GENERAL TABLE OF ALL THE ITALIAN
VERBS; on a large sheet of imperial paper, 3 s

4. NOUVEAU VOCABULAIRE, Français, Anglais, et
Italien, à l'usage des Ecoles, et des Voyageurs, par R. Zotti. Second
edition, 12mo. bound, 6s.

5. TEATRO ITALIANO, o sia Scelta di Commedie e Tragedie, ad uso della gioventù studiosa, sewed, 3 vols. 12mo. 14s.

6. GUICCIARDINI, le Istorie, ridotte in compendio da
R. Zotti. 12mo. sewed, 5s.

7. ULTIME LETTERE DI JACOPO ORTIS. 12mo.
boards, 6s.

8. LETTERE DI PAPA GANGANELLI, 2 vols. 12mo.
sewed, 12s.

9. ALFIERI TRAGEDIE, Scelte, sewed, 2 vols. 10s.

10. DANTE, OPERE TUTTE. Head of the Author, by Schiavonetti, 3 vols. 12mo. sewed, 1l. 4s.

11. PETRARCA, IL CANZONIERE, e Vita di Mad. Laura. Heads of Petrarch, by ditto, and of Laura. Fine paper, 3 vols. 12mo. boards, 1l. 4s.

12. PASTOR FIDO, DEL GUARINI. Head of Guarini. Fine paper, 2 vols. 12mo. sewed, 7s. 6d.

13. LA GERUSALEMME LIBERATA, con Note. Head of Tasso, with his Life, and General Index, 2 vols. 12mo. uniform with the above Classics, sewed, 12s.

14. METASTASIO, Opere tutte. Head of the Author, with his Life, &c. 6 vols. sewed, 12mo. 2l. 8s.

15. METASTASIO, Scelte di Opere. 2 vols. sewed, 12s.

16. ARIOSTO, Orlando Furioso. Head of the Author, with his Life, sewed, 12mo. 1l. 4s.

17. DITTO, Castigato, for Young People, 4 vols. 12mo. 1l. 4s.

GERMAN.

EDWARD IN SCOTLAND; or the Night of a Fugitive; an Historical Drama, in Three Acts. By Augustus Von Kotzebue. Adapted to the Hamiltonian System, by Literal, Interlineal, and Explanatory Notes. By J. Underwood. 4s. 6d.

"In this adaptation of a familiar and popular play of *Kotzebue* to the Hamiltonian System, by a literal and interlineal translation, *Mr. Underwood* has rendered a valuable service to the student. The style of the dialogue is so homely—we must not venture to say natural when we are speaking of *Kotzebue*—that a better selection could scarcely have been made of a medium through which to acquire a knowledge of the colloquial language. This volume possesses, independently of its intrinsic excellence as an Hamiltonian translation, other advantages which, although apparently slight, will be found of great advantage to the pupil. The German type is remarkably clear and brilliant, which is rarely the case in works of this description; and the text is printed at the end, along with the translation, in the English character; so that any difficulty which may arise respecting the identification of letters—a difficulty which belongs entirely to the first step in German—may be resolved at once by a reference to the latter part. There are also foot notes to the pages, in which a variety of idiomatic phrases are explained, grammatical peculiarities pointed out, the value, and, in some instances, the etymology of particular words determined, and a great deal of useful information, running current with the subject from which it springs, embodied in the briefest space possible. We recommend this little volume to the attention of students, and may take this opportunity of observing that the objections which have been justly raised against some of the modern plans, by which pupils learn too fast, and lose what they learn as fast as they acquire it, does not apply to works of this kind, nor, indeed, to the *Hamiltonian System*, as it is developed by such judicious teachers as *Mr. Underwood*. The pupil cannot learn too fast by this system, unless it be strained to produce that result, because he can learn only in proportion to the grasp of his capacity, as it is emphatically addressed to his *understanding*, and not to his *memory*. His progress, therefore, must be in an exact ratio with his power of acquisition, which, being constantly exercised, and called back upon his past reading, cannot, if he do justice to himself, be employed in vain."—*Atlas, Sunday, Dec. 27th.*

LATIN BOOKS.

1. SOUTER'S FIRST LATIN-ENGLISH DICTION-
ARY; abridged from Ainsworth, &c. Small 8vo. Price 3s. English-
Latin part, price 2s. 6d.; or both parts done up together, price 5s.

2. FIRST LESSONS in LATIN; consisting of easy and
progressive Selections in Latin Construing. New Edition, with an
Index to supersede the necessity of reference to a Dictionary. By the
Rev. J. Evans. 2s.

3. INTRODUCTION to the WRITING of LATIN EX-
ERCISES; containing easy Exercises on all the Declinable, with co-
piously arranged Lists of the Indeclinable Parts of Speech; on a plan
which cannot possibly fail to secure to the Pupil a thorough understanding of the Principles of Grammar, by a gradual Development of
the Rules, in a series of Examples strictly appropriate and purely classical. The radical Latin is interlined throughout, to prevent the necessity of any Reference, except to the Grammar; and the whole so varied,
that most of the leading Verbs in the Language are introduced under
their respective Conjugations. Adapted to the Eton Grammar. By
James Mitchell. New Edition, greatly improved, enlarged, and corrected throughout. 1s. 6d.

4. FAMILIAR and PRACTICAL LATIN GRAMMAR,
on an entirely new and simple method of Teaching the Rudiments of the
Latin Tongue. By A. C. Abeille. Part I., price 1s. 6d. Part II., 1s. 6d.
Both Parts together, 2s. 6d.

"The design of Mr. Abeille's 'Practical Latin Grammar' is one of the best we
ever met with," &c.—*Spectator.*

"The 'Familiar Practical Latin Grammar,' by M. A. C. Abeille, instructs us in a
method of teaching the Latin Rudiments very simply and effectually."—*Literary
Gazette, April 2d.*

"A very useful elementary treatise; remarkable for its simplicity and conciseness."
—*The Sun, April 21st.*

See also *The Educational Magazine*, No. XV., March, 1836. Pp. 189-90.

5. LECTIONES SELECTÆ. By Rev. J. Adams. 18mo. 1s. bd.

6. SELECT LATIN LESSONS, rendered into English,
to be re-translated into Latin. By Rev. J. Adams. 18mo. 1s. bound.

7. THE LONDON ENGLISH and LATIN VOCABU-
LARY. By J. Greenwood. New Edition, revised and corrected by
N. Howard. 18mo. 1s. 6d. bound.

8. QUESTIONS for EXAMINATION in the ETON
LATIN GRAMMAR. By the Rev. J. Evans. 1s.

9. THE FABLES of PHÆDRUS, First and Second
Books; in Five Parts.

Part I. contains the Text itself of the First and Second Books.

The *Second Part* contains the Words of the Author according to their
Grammatical Construction, the proper English added to, and the Con-
cord and Government of, each Word in the First Book only; with
Figures referring to corresponding Figures in The Index of Rules for
Concord and Government in the Fifth Part.

The *Third Part* contains a literal Translation of the Second Book
only; every Latin Word being followed by its proper English in Italics.

The *Fourth Part* contains an Index of all the Substantives and Verbs
in the First Book, showing the Genders of the former, and the Preterperfect Tenses and Supines of the latter; with Figures referring likewise
to corresponding Figures in The Index of Rules, &c.

The *Fifth Part* contains an Index, referring to the Rules of Grammar, for the Concord and Government of all the Words which occur in
the First Book, for the Preterperfect Tenses and Supines of Verbs, and
for the Genders of Nouns; with two or three first Words of each Rule,
and the Page in which that Rule is to be found in The Common Accidence, published by John Ward or Richard Mant; or in Ward's, the
Eton, or Valpy's Latin Grammars: the Figure prefixed answering to
those which occur in the Second Part or Grammatical Construction.

Every Latin Word of more than two Syllables, in the Second, Third,
Fourth, and Fifth Parts, is accented, for the Use of young Beginners
in the Latin Tongue. By Richard Mant, D.D., formerly Master of the
Free Grammar-School, Southampton. Fifth Edition, corrected. 2s. 6d.

10. PHÆDRI FABULÆ. A new Edition, in 12mo.
with many improvements. By John Stirling, D.D. 3s. 6d. bound.

11. EUTOPII HISTORIÆ BREVIARUM. By J. Stirling. New Edition, 12mo. 3s. 6d. bound.

12. AN INTRODUCTION to the MAKING of LATIN.
New Edition, by J. Clark. 3s. 6d.

13. CLARK'S CORDERIUS. 12mo. 1s. 6d.

14. LOGGAN'S COLLOQUIES of CORDERY, Latin
and English. 12mo. 2s. bound.

15. CLARK'S CORNELIUS NEPOS. 12mo. 4s. bound.

16. BALLANTYNE'S INTRODUCTION to LATIN
READING. 12mo. 3s. 6d. bound.

17. BEZA'S LATIN TESTAMENT. 12mo. 1s.6d. bound.

18. COLLECTANEA LATINA; or Easy Construing Les-
sons from the best Latin Authors. By the Rev. W. Allen. bd. 3s.

19. ELLIS'S LATIN EXERCISES. 12mo. 3s. 6d. bound.

20. A KEY to ditto. 12mo. 3s. 6d. bound.

21. A KEY; or, LITERAL TRANSLATION to VALPY's LATIN DELECTUS. 12mo. 3s. 6d.

22. STUDIA METRICA; or, an Introduction to the Composition of Latin Hexameter and Pentameter, Alcaic and Sapphic Verse. By J. W. Underwood. 12mo. 2s. 6d. bound.

23. A KEY to the above. By the same Author. 2s. 6d.

24. ETYMOTONIA; containing Principles of Classical Accentuation, and intended as a Guide to the right Pronunciation of Greek and Latin Words, and of all Scientific Terms whether Classical or Barbarous, including the Ancient Proper Names, and such modern Proper Names as are written with a Latin Termination. By means of a Terminational Arrangement, a few Easy Rules comprise more than nine-tenths of the subject. By Æneas M'Intyre, LL. D., Fellow of the Linnæan Society, &c. Price 5s. 6d.

25. CÆSAR, IN USUM DELPHINI. 8vo. bound. 12s.

26. CICERONIS ORATIONES, IN USUM DELPHINI. 8vo. 10s. 6d. bound.

27. JUVENALIS et PERSII FLACCI SATIRÆ, in USUM DELPHINI. 8vo. 9s. bound.

28. C. SALLUSTII CRISPI de CATALINÆ CONJU-RATIONE deque BELLO JUGURTHINO LIBRI. Cod. scriptis simul impressisque quadraginta Amplius Collatis, recensuit, atque adnotationibus illustravit. H. E. Allen. 7s. 6d.
" Mr. Allen has given an edition that we do not believe a dozen Englishmen could equal ; exhibiting, as it does, the very rare union of the patient research of the scholar, combined with the delicate perception of the man of taste."—*Gentleman's Magazine.*

29. OVIDII METAMORPHOSES, in USUM DEL-PHINI. 8vo. 10s. 6d. bound.

30. OVIDII EPISTOLÆ, ditto. 8vo. 8s. bound.

31. VIRGIL, IN USUM DELPHINI. 8vo. bound. 11s.

32. VIRGIL, with a Prose Translation by Davidson. 2 vol. 8vo. 21s. boards.

33. TYRONNIS THESAURUS; or, Entick's Latin and English Dictionary. Square 12mo. 5s. 6d. bound.

34. ENTICK'S ENGLISH and LATIN DICTIONARY; containing all the Words and Phrases proper for Reading the Classics in both Languages; to which is added, a Latin and English Dictionary. By Wm. Craklet, A.M. A new Edition, corrected by the Rev. M. G. Sargant, B.A. Square 12mo. 9s. bound.

35. AINSWORTH'S LATIN and ENGLISH and ENG-
LISH and LATIN DICTIONARY. By Morell. 8vo. new Edition,
corrected and improved by Dr. Ross. 15s. bound.

---

1. THE FOUR ORATIONS of CICERO against CA-
TALINE, with an Interlineal Translation and Notes, adapted to the
Hamiltonian System. By J. Underwood. 4s.

2. THE MEDICAL STUDENTS' PRACTICAL and
THEORETICAL GUIDE to the TRANSLATION and COMPO-
SITION of LATIN PRESCRIPTIONS; with an Explanatory Latin
Grammar, written in a familiar style, together with a Text Book and
Exercises; calculated to make the Learner thoroughly acquainted with
the Verbal and Grammatical Analysis of the Pharmacopœia, Prescrip-
tions, &c. By J. W. Underwood, author of interlineal Translations of
Hippocrates, Celsus, Gregory's Conspectus, &c. &c. 18mo. 5s. 6d.

This Work has been written expressly with the view of enabling Medical Students
and persons engaged in compounding Medicines, to gain an ample acquaintance with
the words usually met with in Prescriptions, and at the same time to acquire an accurate knowledge of the rules by which those words are connected, so as to form sentences. At the commencement of the Work will be found a Grammar of the Latin
Language, written in a concise, clear, and popular style; after this will follow a
Text-Book and Exercise Book, each of which will serve as a Key to the other. Every
example introduced into this Work will have an immediate connexion with the object
in view, and will direct itself to the every-day associations of the Class for whose benefit it was written. The author has, throughout the book, afforded frequent repetitions
of the same words and phrases, and has endeavoured, as much as possible, to facilitate
the process of mental association; for long and extensive experience, as a Teacher, has
convinced him that these two principles are the most potent for the acquirement of a
language.

3. CELSUS DE MEDICINA, with literal and Interlineal Translation, adapted to the Hamiltonian System. By J. W.
Underwood. 3 vols. in cloth. 20s.

₀ The Eight Books complete, Latin only. 12mo. in cloth. 6s.

4. GREGORY'S CONSPECTUS MEDICINÆ THEO-
RETICÆ, with interlineal Translations; on the Plan of CELSUS.
By J. W. Underwood. 2 vols. in cloth. 16s.

5. THE APHORISMS of HIPPOCRATES; containing
the original Greek, with an interlineal and literal Translation, followed
by a free Version and Notes. By J. W. Underwood. In 1 vol. 12mo.
handsomely bound in cloth. 9s.

GREEK BOOKS.

1. EASY GREEK EXERCISES; for the Use of the lower Forms; on the plan of the Eton Latin Minora: with a Greek and English Lexicon of every Work in the Book; forming the most easy Introduction to Greek composition ever published. Second Edition, with an entirely new Lexicon. By the Rev. Wm. Mosely, A.M., LL.D. 2s. 6d. bound.

No Work has before appeared which affords equal assistance in acquiring the art of writing Greek.

2. ÆSOPO FABULÆ, ad usum Alumnorum præcipue sub mea Tutela accommodatæ; sed etiam, si placuerit, aliorum. Cum Notis et Lexico quas scripsit et collegit Rev. T. Andrews, A.M. New edition. 3s. 6d.

3. A KEY, or, literal Translation to Dr. Valpy's Greek Delectus. 12mo. 2s. 6d.

4. SCHRIVELII LEXICON MANUALE GRÆCO-LATINUM, et Latino-Græcum. New Edition, 8vo. 12s. bound.

5. HEDERICK'S GREEK LEXICON. 4to. £2. 5s.

6. HOMER'S ILIAD; translated into English Prose. 2 vols. 8vo. 16s. boards.

7. HOMER'S ODYSSEY; translated into English Prose. 8vo. 16s.

8. THE MODERN GREEK INTERPRETER; a Series of Dialogues in modern Greek, English, and Italian. By M. C. and T. Macri, of Athens. 3s. 6d. half-bound.

9. THE MODERN GREEK GRAMMAR of JULIUS DAVID, late Professor in the Greek College of Scio: rendered into English by the late Rev. G. Winnock, A.B., of Magdalen Hall, Oxford, and Chaplain to the Forces in the Ionian Islands. 5s. boards.

To persons interested in the affairs of Greece, and to those desirous of acquiring a knowledge of the modern language of that country, the above two Works will materially increase their means of understanding the same.

DR. TRUSLER'S USEFUL PUBLICATIONS.

~~~~~~~~~~~~

1. TRUSLER'S SURE and EASY WAY to PRO-
LONG LIFE, &c. A New and Sixth Edition, (a test of merit,) much
enlarged. 2 vol. 8vo. 10s.

The Author pledges his hard-earned character, that the reader will
not grudge its cost, as it will be the means of saving many a torturing
disease, many an apothecary's bill, and many a nauseous draught.

By ample directions here given, founded on the best medical practice,
the most respectable authorities, and experience in various cases mentioned, all ages (none too late,) will learn to avoid diseases; to cure
them without physic; to prolong life beyond its usual limits, (as he
himself has done;) the young to prevent the infirmities of age; the old,
labouring under them, to relieve themselves, and pass out of life free
from any bodily pain.

Here is also a never failing remedy for the cramp; and, fanciful as it
may seem, ladies will find an effectual mode of increasing personal
beauty and prolonging it.

2. NEW SYSTEM of DOMESTIC MANAGE-
MENT, 12mo. 5s. A Book which ought to be in the hands of every
good managing Housewife or Housekeeper.

3. LEGAL and USEFUL INFORMATION, on
every species of real Property, Estates, Houses, Annuities, Mines, &c.,
with a legal mode of making twenty per cent. for the use of money,
without risk; necessary to Landed Proprietors, Solicitors, and all who
have any concern in the transfer of Property. 4s. bound.
Very useful to Students and Public Speakers.

4. The COUNTRY LAWYER, a Book of Reference,
on all Legal Subjects a Gentleman in the Country has occasion to consult. 3s.

5. TRUSLER'S CHRONOLOGY, Vol. III. 12mo.
5s. An EPITOME of this, that will lie in a pocket-book. 3s.

6. An ENGLISH ACCIDENCE; teaches correct
Reading and Speaking, without making Grammar a Study. 1s. 6d.

7. FIRST FOUR RULES of ARITHMETIC, adapted
to the capacity of Girls; all that is necessary for them to learn; and
needs no Master. 1s. 6d.

8. TRUSLER'S FAMILY TABLES for all purposes, saves all Calculations. 1s. 6d.

9. The PROGRESS of MAN, from the Cradle to the Grave, and of SOCIETY, from its Infancy; in four parts, illustrated by 108 well-designed wood engravings. "Come, Boy, learn to be wise." 5s. bound.

Part I. gradually opens the mind, tracing man from Infancy, through Boyhood, shews the utility and wisdom of all sportive exercises, every branch of Education, and the obligations we are under to Parents, Nurses, and Tutors.

Part II. carries him on through Manhood, as a Husband, Father, and Citizen; shews the wisdom of God in his Structure, develops the uses and powers of all his faculties, with his duty to improve and not abuse them.

Part III. describes him in a state of Nature, next in Civilisation; gives an insight into the nature and utility of all Manufactures, of Trade and Commerce, and shews how all are well contrived to his comfort and happiness.

Part IV. gives him a sufficient knowledge of the Elements, their appearances, uses, the powerful effects of Nature, and all its operations; the blessings and scourges of Heaven, and the provision and punishment of Laws, for the benefit of Society.

A celebrated Author speaks thus highly of it.—" *There can be but one opinion with those who have fortunately introduced this Book into their families, viz. that if any one instructive Book be preferable to another, it is this. It suits all ages and both sexes. Children learning to read from it, must acquire an early knowledge of everything, and it amuses so much that it is never out of the hands of my Children.*"—*G. CUMBERLAND.*

10. INSTRUCTIVE PROVERBS, paraphrased and exemplified by scenes in real life, with fifty well-designed wood engravings. 5s. bound.

11. The SAME in VERSE of all measures, with Rules for reading it, teaching youth to read poetry well, which very few can do. 3s. 6d. bound.

12. A COMPENDIUM of USEFUL KNOWLEDGE, on all subjects, particularly Religion, Natural History, Trade, Commerce, Army, Navy, and the Constitution of this Country, &c., with an Epitome of English History; enabling youth to converse on all subjects. Question and Answer. 3s. 6d.

13. A COMPENDIUM of SACRED HISTORY, Question and Answer, from Dr. STACKHOUSE's History of the Bible. 2 vol. 7s. 6d.

14. PRINCIPLES of POLITENESS. This teaches polite manners and a knowledge of mankind, and contains very essential advice to young women, on their first outset in life. 5s. bound.

15. INSTRUCTIVE ESSAYS; (6s. 6d.) addressed to young men of Fortune, (under the Title of a WARM APPEAL against the Disturbers of their own quiet and that of others,) as follows: The True Gentleman.—Rank.—Greatness of Mind.—Truth.—Honour.—Marriage.—Opinion of the World.—Competency.—Extravagance and Gaming.—Economy.—Running in Debt.—Almsgiving.—Pleasure of Bestowing.—Litigation proved Antichristian.—Value of a good Name. —Independence.

16. BLACKSTONE'S COMMENTARIES abridged, calculated to impress the Laws of this Country on the Mind. 4s. 6d.

" A Knowledge of the Laws is an essential part of a liberal Education, and no man is safe without it."—BLACKSTONE.

17. MODERN TIMES, or the ADVENTURES of GABRIEL OUTCAST, a satirical Novel, in the manner of Gil Blas. 3 vol. 12mo. with 12 copper-plates. 16s.

18. LIFE; or the ADVENTURES of WILLIAM RAMBLE, Esq. on the plan of the above. 3 vol. 5 plates. 14s.

The Reviews of the Times spoke highly of these Novels, deeming the Author the " very Heemskirk of Novelists." They teach more Knowledge of the arts and deceptions of the world than twenty years' experience.

" Those who have not read the Adventures of Gabriel Outcast, would do well to spend a few idle hours in the perusal of this useful and entertaining Novel."

See Baron Knigge's Practical Philosophy. Vol. II. page 231.

19. THE CHRISTIAN'S AID in SEARCHING the SCRIPTURES for his FAITH and SALVATION. 3s. 6d.

Here the mysteries of Religion, viz. Regeneration, Election, Justifying Faith, &c. are unfolded and made clearly intelligible to the most common capacity; and the Athanasian Creed freed from any supposed inconsistency: together with a copious explanation of the Liturgy of the Church of England, which few know the nature of, but which all should well understand.

A proper book to be given away to the lower order of the people by those who wish to do good to mankind. It points out such chapters as require most attention.

20. THE MASTER'S LAST and BEST GIFT to his APPRENTICE in his Outset in Life, pointing out his Way to Wealth and Reputation. 2s. 6d.

This Book treats fully of the whole Art of Trading, Shopkeeping, Capital, Situation, Appearance, Civility, Stock, Profits, Speculation, Servants, Apprentices, Marriage, Housekeeping, and other Expenses, Economy; Goodwill, modes of doing Business and of carrying on extensive concerns even without a Capital or Loan, danger of Securities, &c. An attention to which must, in a few years, realise a good fortune, and is worth the attention of tradesmen long in business.

* Printed by J. and C. Adlard, Bartholomew Close.